Selecting and Using
Hand Tools

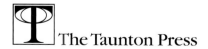
The Editors of
Fine Woodworking

The Taunton Press

The Taunton Press
Inspiration for hands-on living®

The Taunton Press, Inc., 63 South Main Street, PO Box 5506, Newtown, CT 06470-5506
e-mail: tp@taunton.com

Jacket/Cover design: Susan Fazekas
Interior design: Susan Fazekas
Layout: Cathy Cassidy
Front Cover Photographer: Timothy Sams, courtesy *Fine Woodworking,*
© The Taunton Press, Inc.
Back Cover Photographers: (clockwise from top left) Boyd Hagen, courtesy *Fine Woodworking,* © The Taunton Press, Inc.; Alec Waters, courtesy *Fine Woodworking,* © The Taunton Press, Inc.; Charley Robinson, courtesy *Fine Woodworking,* © The Taunton Press, Inc.

The New Best of Fine Woodworking® is a trademark of The Taunton Press, Inc., registered in the U.S. Patent and Trademark Office.

Library of Congress Cataloging-in-Publication Data
Selecting and using hand tools / The editors of Fine woodworking.
    p. cm. -- (The new best of fine woodworking)
 ISBN 1-56158-783-4
 1. Woodworking tools. I. Fine woodworking. II. Series.
 TT186.S38 2005
 684'.082--dc22

                        2005001232
Printed in the United States of America
10 9 8 7 6 5 4 3 2 1

The following manufacturers/names appearing in *Selecting and Using Hand Tools* are trademarks: Allway®, Bailey®, Bedrock®, Bosch®, Bridge City Tool Works®, Brown & Sharpe®, DeWalt®, Formby's®, Greenlee®, Henry Taylor Tools®, Lamello®, Lie-Nielson®, Lucite®, Marples®, Millers Falls®, Minwax®, Mitutoyo®, Nicholson®, Plexiglas®, Record®, Stanley®, Starrett®, Veritas®, Waterlox®, WD-40®, Weld-On®, Woodcraft®, X-Acto®

Working wood is inherently dangerous. Using hand or power tools improperly or ignoring safety practices can lead to permanent injury or even death. Don't try to perform operations you learn about here (or elsewhere) unless you're certain they are safe for you. If something about an operation doesn't feel right, don't do it. Look for another way. We want you to enjoy the craft, so please keep safety foremost in your mind whenever you're in the shop.

Acknowledgments

Special thanks to the authors, editors,
art directors, copy editors, and other
staff members of *Fine Woodworking* who
contributed to the development of the
articles in this book.

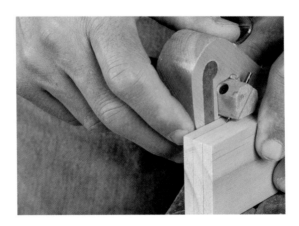

Contents

Introduction

I have about 100 times more money invested in machines than in hand tools, but it's the hand tools I cherish most. Unlike a machine, a well-tuned hand plane or razor-sharp chisel allows me to engage with wood in a personal, satisfying way. It's like driving a car versus taking a walk. One method gets you there faster, but the latter allows you to see every ripple in the landscape.

Because of our fast-paced lives we are thankful for machines; otherwise we would not do as many projects promised to our family or to our clients. But at some point all woodworking requires the use of some hand tools. Although you may not think of them as such, a ruler, a marking knife, and a square are hand tools that are essential for layout as well as for machine setup. Knowing how to choose and use these tools will make you a better woodworker.

There are times when a handplane or chisel comes in handy, even if you work mostly with machines. Nothing pares an oversized tenon as accurately as a fine swipe across its cheek with a shoulder plane. To shape curvy parts like a ball-and-claw foot, you will need files, rasps, and rifflers.

To do honest period work, you must cut your dovetails by hand. A fine-tooth saw and chisel will have to be employed and

eventually sharpened to continue working. For certain details, like a narrow bead with a fine quirk or groove, you are best off making your own simple tool, a scratch stock.

These and other hand-tool articles are excerpted here from the pages of *Fine Woodworking* magazine. Once you start using more of these tools you will see your work reach a higher level of refinement and realize that the extra time spent doing hand work is well worth every minute.

—Anatole Burkin, editor of *Fine Woodworking* magazine.

Four Tools You Shouldn't Overlook

BY MIKE DUNBAR

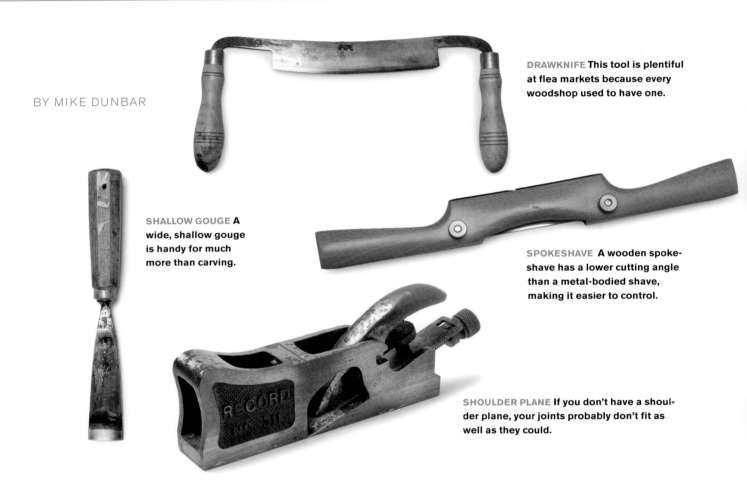

DRAWKNIFE This tool is plentiful at flea markets because every woodshop used to have one.

SHALLOW GOUGE A wide, shallow gouge is handy for much more than carving.

SPOKESHAVE A wooden spokeshave has a lower cutting angle than a metal-bodied shave, making it easier to control.

SHOULDER PLANE If you don't have a shoulder plane, your joints probably don't fit as well as they could.

You have finally set up your shop just the way you want it. You've built your workbench. You have bought your tablesaw, thickness planer, jointer, and bandsaw. On your shop wall you have sharp chisels, a dovetail saw, and smoothing and block planes. You feel equipped to handle any project, but you may be overlooking a few very useful hand tools.

I find the following four tools indispensable: drawknife, shallow gouge, spokeshave, and shoulder plane. The first two are used generally for roughing; the others are used for fine work. However, all are so handy that it would be impossible to describe all of their uses. Put them to work, and you will soon come up with jobs I haven't thought of. As a bonus, only the shoulder plane will cost more than $100. The other three tools are priced closer to $50.

With some practice, hand tools like these are faster than machines, easier to control, and pose less danger to a semi-finished workpiece. While they cut a little more slowly than a bandsaw or router, they don't require any setup or test cuts. Just pick up the tool, do what you need, and move on. Frequently, the job is over before you could set a fence and flick a switch.

Drawknife

There is only one explanation for why old drawknives are so plentiful. Until this last generation, every woodworker owned one. The tool is so useful that I cannot imagine a shop without one. It is used for quick stock removal along the grain and across the grain and for concave and convex curves. It will cut away heavy amounts of wood far faster than a bandsaw can.

Here are a couple of tips on using a drawknife. It is a slicing tool, not a two-handled hatchet. Hold it askew and draw the edge through the wood the way a butcher slices meat. You will be amazed at how effortlessly and cleanly it works. Use the drawknife with the bezel (the ground surface often called the bevel) and manufacturer's stamp up. Many woodworkers use the knife upside down, because they think it gives them more control. However, because they cannot take a heavy chip in this position, they sacrifice the tool's most important ability: fast stock removal. Far better that you learn to use the knife the proper way. You will be able to take paper-thin shavings that rival those made with a plane or hog off slices as thick as your finger. The drawknife can be used to shape complex contours, such as those on chair parts, or to quickly remove waste, such as when a turner cuts away the corners of a square blank before mounting it on the lathe. I

often use my drawknife in an unconventional way. If I have a crooked or irregular board that needs one edge jointed straight, the drawknife gets me a straight edge as quickly as a bandsaw. First, I snap a chalkline, and then, after determining the grain direction so I am working with it rather than against it, I use the knife as a lever, prying loose the waste close to the line. A few passes over the jointer and I have a straight edge.

Buy an old drawknife or a good replica made by a smith who understands the tool. Most modern knives are ground as steeply as chisels, and this edge will not slice like a knife.

#3 Sweep-35mm Gouge

Not a day goes by that the #3 sweep-35mm gouge is not in my hands many times. The tool handles rough stock removal in places where the drawknife is too large. Depending on the size of the job, it can be driven with the heel of my palm or with a mallet. The gouge trims joints in far less time than a saw does. It whittles pins and wedges for mortise-and-tenon joints, and because it is so constantly at hand, I use it in place of a jackknife. Because its edge is a shallow curve, it is far less likely to dig in

USED BEZEL-SIDE UP, the drawknife quickly slices away material. The tool is held at an angle and pulled across the work to create a shearing action. Here, a blank is prepared for turning.

A WIDE GOUGE with a shallow
sweep can whittle or trim. Here,
the author uses his favorite
version–#3 sweep-35mm wide–
to pin the joints in a frame-and-
panel door.

and scar your work than a flat chisel, making it ideal for trimming pegs flush.

At a *Fine Woodworking* conference,
"Working Wood in the 18th Century" at
Colonial Williamsburg, I was surprised to
see the center's master cabinetmaker, Mack
Headley, pull out a gouge nearly identical
to mine. Driving it with a mallet, he used it
to rough out the concave curves of a crest
rail on a Queen Anne chair. This is a job
most of us would have done on a bandsaw,
but Headley did it with the part already
glued in place by blending the contours of
the rail smoothly into the back posts. The
gouge Headley used was a modern copy of
an old one archeologists dug up in Williamsburg at the site of an 18th-century cabinetmaker's shop. Those old boys also knew
how handy this tool is.

When I'm shaping parts, fitting tenons,
or whittling pins, I usually hold the chisel
handle against my chest and pull the wood
toward the blade. This gives me more control, and it's safer when working around
other people.

A SHARP SPOKESHAVE fairs complex contours.
Hold the tool near its body for better support and
control of the blade. Here, the author shaves away
bandsaw marks on a chair leg.

Wooden Spokeshave

This tool is as close to magical as any you
will ever use. It is the equivalent of using a
photo-editing program to work on a picture. You can smooth curves and blend elements together.

Do not confuse the wooden shave with the metal tool that bears the same name. They have very little in common. The wooden shave's blade is set nearly parallel to the sole with the bezel up, so it has a low cutting angle. This makes it ideal for end grain. A sharp shave will take clean shavings from end grain that hold together like those taken from edge grain.

A wooden spokeshave is ideal in many of the situations where woodworkers would use a rasp, such as cabriole legs, but the shave leaves a surface so smooth that it is almost ready for finish. Often a spokeshave is used to refine the larger facets left by a drawknife or gouge.

A shave can be pulled—when whittling—but it is primarily a pushing tool. While its handles seem to imply that you grip them, you should instead hold the central body of the tool between your fingers with your thumb behind the blade. This position makes it a lot easier to control.

When setting up your shave, cock the blade so that the cutting edge is higher on one side than on the other. This gives you high, medium, and low settings all in one. When you need to take a shaving of a different thickness, just move the shave to a different point along the edge. It saves a lot of time making adjustments.

Shoulder Plane

No matter how precise your joinery, you will have to make fine adjustments. Often, there is no practical way to do this with machines. That's why every shop should have a shoulder plane. This plane has an extremely narrow mouth, which allows it to make cuts so fine that the chips just crumble to dust.

As its name implies, a shoulder plane can be used to snug up the shoulders on mortise-and-tenon joints. But the tool is far more versatile than that. Because its mouth and

A SHOULDER PLANE is unmatched at trimming joinery. The tool works all the way into corners and can take very fine shavings.

blade are as wide as its sole, it can reach completely into a corner to trim a rabbet joint or the shoulders on a tongue-and-groove joint. Many woodworkers also use a shoulder plane to shave away the cheeks of a tenon to create a perfect friction fit. (While doing this job, use the plane to chamfer the end of the tenon so that it slides in easily.) It is also ideal for truing, trimming, or smoothing the flat fillets on moldings.

Shoulder planes are not cheap, and I would be leery of one that is. However, you will never wear one out, and it will make an important difference in the quality of your work.

Try these hand tools. Each of the four is sure to speed up and refine your work.

MIKE DUNBAR is a contributing editor to *Fine Woodworking* magazine.

Shop on the Go

BY MARIO RODRIGUEZ

I often find myself far from a well-equipped shop, and when I reach my destination I typically need a good collection of woodworking tools that can help me tackle anything from basic joinery to furniture repair.

I've been a cabinetmaker for a long time, and I own lots of tools. When I travel, I can't lug everything, so I pare down my collection to the tools that give me the best results with the least weight and bulk. Although I routinely use a variety of stationary power tools when they are available, my travel kit allows me to make almost any small project from scratch when they are not. In my travels I've discovered that this set is really all I need and would serve as a good set of essentials for any shop.

In addition to being compact and portable, tools must have three qualities: each must be effective, versatile, and of good quality. Effectiveness means a tool must be well designed and well balanced, easy to adjust, comfortable to use, and easy to sharpen and maintain. Versatile means that it should perform more than one task. Quality is important, too. This is about more than appearance: Top-quality tools work better.

Everything in my travel kit meets these criteria, with one exception: a set of completely useless screwdrivers my daughter proudly gave to me on Father's Day when she was seven years old. I never go anywhere without them.

Key Personal Tools Include Planes and Chisels

Personal tools are ones that I always carry. I never leave them lying around, and (sorry, buddy) I rarely lend them to anyone.

I used to laugh at people who bundled their pets in little jackets. Now I pack my planes in special socks. I carry four planes: a

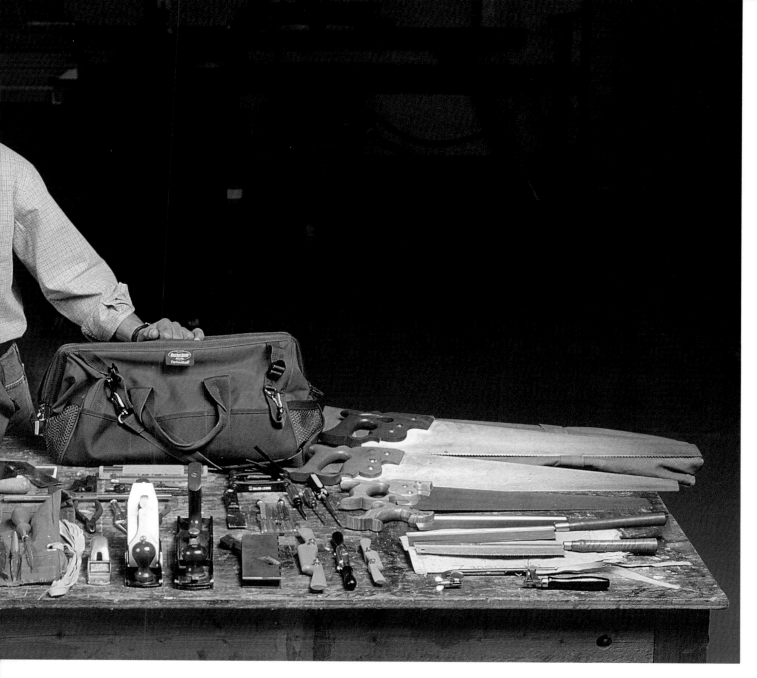

A TRAVEL KIT of carefully chosen tools keeps a veteran cabinet-maker at work away from home.

Planes

Rodriguez's traveling collection of tools includes four planes (from left): a block plane, a low-angle jack plane, a No. 4 smoothing plane, and a ¾-in. shoulder plane that he made.

Chisels

Paring chisels, from ⅛ in. to 2 in. wide, are protected by a heavy canvas roll during the rigors of travel. The kit also includes a turned carver's-style mallet.

low-angle jack, a block plane, a No. 4 smoothing plane, and a shoulder plane. Three of my planes are made by Lie-Nielsen®, where I work part-time as a consultant. The planes are well made, but they are expensive. In most cases, you could substitute another brand, such as Record® or Stanley®.

The low-angle jack plane is a copy of the Stanley No. 62. It is long enough to serve as a jointer yet short enough to double as a smoothing plane. It can cut with the grain or perpendicular to the grain, and it even handles end grain. It also works on very dense woods such as bird's-eye maple. Like most woodworkers, I can't do without a block plane. Mine is a Lie-Nielsen No. 103, but good block planes also are made by Stanley and Record. A No. 4 smoothing plane is rightfully regarded as an all-purpose bench plane. I use mine to smooth and flatten short and narrow pieces, to clean up edges, and to remove saw marks and other surface blemishes. The last plane in my kit is a ¾-in. shoulder plane. I made this one myself, modeling it after one from the tool chest of famed 19th-century cabinetmaker Duncan Phyfe. Unlike other planes, a shoulder plane's blade extends the full width of the plane body, making it useful for trimming rabbets, tenons, and shoulders. A good substitute is the Stanley No. 92.

I carry six paring chisels—⅛ in., ¼ in., ½ in., ¾ in., 1 in and 2 in.—although it would be possible to get by without the ⅛-in. and 2-in. chisels. I also bring a ¼-in. mortise chisel that doubles as a heavy-duty bench chisel (and I use my ½-in. chisel as a burnisher for my scrapers). I think Marples'® Blue Chip is a good brand at a good price. And I have a small turned mallet for whacking chisels.

I admit to having a weakness for spokeshaves. I love the way they look and handle. Because they don't take up much room, I carry several, including 1½-in. and 2-in. models. If you prefer the more common cast-iron style with a flat sole, either the Stanley No. 51 or the Record No. 501 will do nicely. Flat card scrapers don't take up much room, either, but they are great for smoothing surfaces, removing plane tracks, and scraping finishes. I carry several.

Layout and Marking Tools

I made my own marking knife. It has a slender, pointed blade and a full handle custom-shaped to fit my hand. It is very handy for scribing clean lines, scribing dove-

Spokeshaves and Scrapers

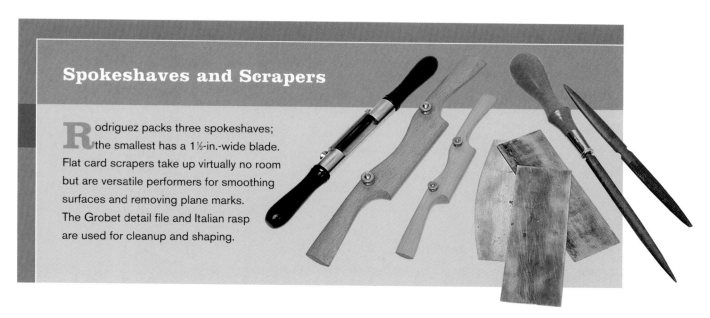

Rodriguez packs three spokeshaves; the smallest has a 1½-in.-wide blade. Flat card scrapers take up virtually no room but are versatile performers for smoothing surfaces and removing plane marks. The Grobet detail file and Italian rasp are used for cleanup and shaping.

tail pins, trimming veneer, sharpening pencils, and even removing splinters. I use an old Reed marking gauge that is no longer made, but Starrett® makes a similar model.

A 12-in. combination square is essential for checking 90-degree and 45-degree angles and for general layout work. Although a 6-in. square would be more compact and accomplish the same basic function as a 12-in. one, I prefer the bigger model because the base is sturdier and the ruler is longer. I think the extra capacity offsets the added weight. A 3-in. engineer's square is useful for checking the squareness of plane blades and chisel edges and for laying out joints.

A sliding T-bevel makes it easy to lay out and copy angles. I use a compact Shinwa model that folds down to the size of a ballpoint pen. A small compass is used for drawing circles and curves and also for scribing trim or the edge of a cabinet that fits against an irregular or tapered surface.

Tools for Filing and Sharpening

I always have 6-in. and 8-in. mill files and sometimes a 10-in. file as well. I use them not only for jointing scrapers and sawteeth

Layout and Marking Tools

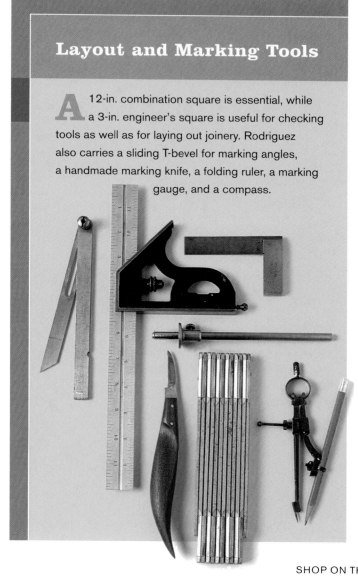

A 12-in. combination square is essential, while a 3-in. engineer's square is useful for checking tools as well as for laying out joinery. Rodriguez also carries a sliding T-bevel for marking angles, a handmade marking knife, a folding ruler, a marking gauge, and a compass.

but also for filing down nail heads and removing burrs from metal tools and parts. In a pinch, these files also can be used on wood to obtain a smooth finish, for cutting light chamfers, and for flushing the protruding ends of dovetails.

A Grobet detail file is a tapered, half-round file originally designed for carving wax in the jewelry trade. One end is used for rough work, and the other is for fine work. I use it for cleaning up carvings, for trimming veneer, and sometimes as a lathe tool. A companion to the Grobet is a 6-in. Italian rasp, which has a compact design for fine shaping. It cuts more aggressively than the Grobet, but the cut and the finish can be controlled by how much pressure is applied to the work.

Because I sharpen my own saws, I also carry a good selection of saw files, from a 4-in. double extra-tapered slim for my dovetail saws up to a 6-in. extra slim for my crosscut saw.

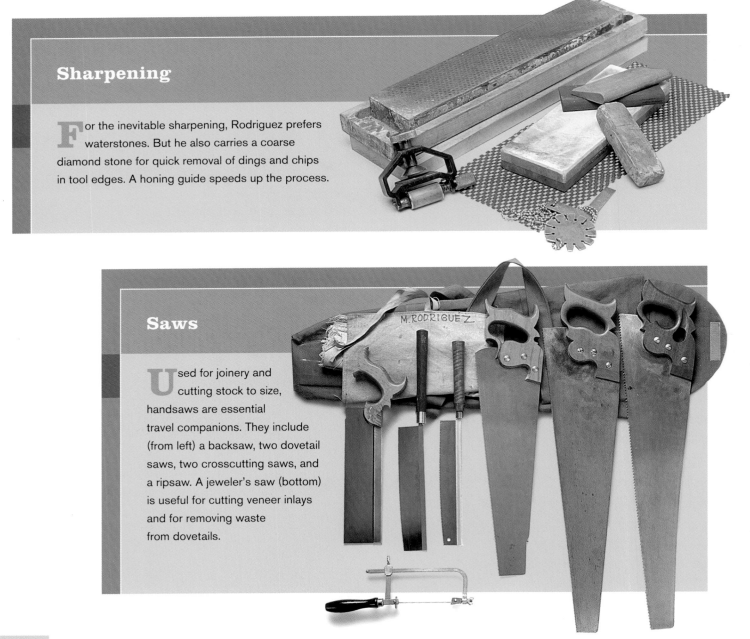

Sharpening

For the inevitable sharpening, Rodriguez prefers waterstones. But he also carries a coarse diamond stone for quick removal of dings and chips in tool edges. A honing guide speeds up the process.

Saws

Used for joinery and cutting stock to size, handsaws are essential travel companions. They include (from left) a backsaw, two dovetail saws, two crosscutting saws, and a ripsaw. A jeweler's saw (bottom) is useful for cutting veneer inlays and for removing waste from dovetails.

Sharpening is a fact of life, and I like to have a 1,000/6,000 combination stone on hand. I prefer waterstones over oilstones. I also like to have a coarse diamond stone with me. It's dead flat and cuts quickly, and it's helpful for removing dings and chips that are too much for the 1,000/6,000 stone. A Veritas® honing guide may not be essential (some woodworkers refer to these jigs as "training wheels"), but it helps me restore dull edges quickly without thinking too hard about it.

Saws and Odds and Ends

Handsaws are fundamental and especially important if you don't have access to a tablesaw or chopsaw. I carry six saws: a 10-in. dovetail saw with 18 tpi that I use for general tasks; a 10-in. modified dovetail saw that I've refiled from a crosscut to an 11-tpi rip pattern; a 10-in. backsaw for cutting mortise-and-tenon joints and for crosscutting small boards; two crosscut saws for cutting solid wood and veneered panels; and, finally, a 26-in. ripsaw (5 tpi).

Tools that don't fit any particular category but manage to fill some important niche include a 13-oz. hammer (you must have one hammer); screwdrivers, including a #1 and #2 Phillips and a standard flat tip; a pair of wire clippers (great for clipping off nail heads); a pair of 6-in. locking pliers, indispensable for holding small parts and as a quick-release clamp; a set of folding met-

Odds and Ends

A process of trial and error has helped Rodriguez add a selection of tools that don't fit any particular category but are essential all the same. Among them are screwdrivers, a putty knife, Allen wrenches, magnifiers, and pliers.

Portable Power Tools

Portable power tools increase my speed and accuracy, and I carry several if I have the room. Some brands are tedious and difficult to adjust, and some have fragile plastic parts. Over time, I've come to like Bosch® tools, but you may have your own favorite. Whatever the brand, the tool should not make your work harder than it already is. The power tools I use the most include

- 12-volt cordless drill, that has a good power-to-weight ratio
- barrel-style jigsaw
- 1½-hp router with a soft-start feature
- DeWalt® biscuit joiner (this model comes close to the performance of a Lamello® at a third of the price)
- quad electrical box with an 8-ft. cord.

IF THERE'S ROOM, the kit includes a router, cordless drill, jigsaw, biscuit joiner, and shopmade quad power box.

ric and standard Allen keys; and a flexible 1-in. putty knife for applying epoxy and wood filler.

Special-Purpose Tools

In addition to the tools I carry most of the time, there also is a set of special-purpose tools. I don't need them every day, but they are essential for studio or shop work: a No. 8 jointer plane, because nothing beats the heft and weight of this tool for flattening surfaces or shooting long edges; a saw

vise and saw set; a veneer saw and a veneer hammer; a quad electrical box with an 8-ft. cord (useful for situations where there aren't enough outlets, or where you have to share scarce outlets with other workers); and a jeweler's saw, similar to a coping saw but with a finer blade, which is used to cut veneer inlays and for cleaning waste from dovetails.

MARIO RODRIGUEZ is a contributing editor to *Fine Woodworking* magazine and the author of *Building Fireplace Mantels* (Taunton Press, 2002).

How to Buy Used Hand Tools

BY ROBERT HUBERT JR.

Iwas excited. I had finally saved up a little extra cash to put toward new hand tools for my shop. I gathered up all my dog-eared woodworking catalogs to pick out planes, chisels, and other tools. The shock came when I hit "total" on my calculator; my modest savings would buy only a fraction of the tools I wanted. But thanks to a neighbor who told me about an old plane he had seen at a local flea market, my tool-buying strategy changed.

The next Sunday I bought that plane, a usable Stanley No. 5, for just $15. Three years later, my collection of vintage hand tools has cost me less than half the price of new tools. And here's the best part: By carefully purchasing and reselling a few extra tools for a profit, my tool buying has begun to pay for the rest of my shop.

Preparing for a Tool Hunt

Whether you call them antique tools, vintage tools, or just plain old tools, hunting for used tools requires preparation. The better equipped you are, the better your chances of acquiring high-quality tools at reasonable prices. Here's the systematic approach I use.

Make a tool "want list" for the work you do. Use catalogs to jog your memory of your shop needs. Be specific. Don't just list "bench plane," put down "Stanley No. 3,"

BEHOLD THE LANGUAGE of auctioneer Richard Crane. Most auctioneers initially start the bidding low; later, they'll open items high.

and list whether you want a wood plane or an all-metal one. Being specific will keep you focused and help you avoid buying tools you don't need.

Study the tools you'll be buying. Start by becoming familiar with tool classes and makers. Certain tools, like drawknives, have changed little over the years. Others, like planes, have changed dramatically. One

WISE TOOL PROSPECTORS, armed with want lists and notes, scope out a table of handplanes and box lots of tool parts during the auction preview. A few of the bidders will snatch up bargains at the end of the auction just by outlasting their competitors.

place to learn about hand tools is in original or reprinted owner's manuals and catalogs. Product literature can help you identify a tool as well. In addition, there are books and associations (see Sources on p. 18) that offer a tour of secondhand tools and sellers, as well as supply information about repairing and using old tools. As a beginner, you can go a long way by studying up on Stanley tools alone.

Learn about fair prices and value.

Although you shouldn't completely rely on price guides, current guides can give you ballpark figures for tools. If you're buying for speculation, the guides can tell you how valuable a tool is. Collectors typically look for limited-production tools or tools from unusual makers. Stay away from these tools if you want a bargain tool for woodworking. Always jot down a fair price range for each of the tools on your want list. An entry in my notebook looks something like this: "Jack Plane—prefer Stanley No. 5 w/corrugated sole—$15–$25."

Four Basic Rules for Buying Vintage Tools

As I head into an uncharted used-tool market with my want list in hand and my head full of knowledge, I follow four basic rules.

Rule #1: Thoroughly inspect the tools you're buying. If a tool has many parts, take it apart and examine the pieces. I carry a simple tool-disassembly kit that consists of two screwdrivers, an Allen wrench set, and a pair of pliers. A hidden crack (see the photo on p. 20) can make an old tool useless. Therefore, after you take a tool apart, wipe away grime with a rag. Then, check the tool's stress points. On a plane, the blade area and mouth are susceptible to stress and so is the rear tote (for more on this, see the sidebar on p. 19). On chisels, check for mallet-caused damage and for splits where the tang meets the handle.

Check for missing or substitute parts. Here again, a manual makes it easy to compare a parts list against the actual tool. At the least, a catalog will show a drawing or photo of what the tool should look like. In addition, the tools themselves can reveal where parts are absent. A threaded hole with nothing attached may indicate a missing fence, for example.

THERE ARE OTHER PLACES TO LOOK for secondhand tools besides auctions and flea markets. Here, Hubert asks about a pair of calipers being offered by a tailgate dealer who temporarily has set up shop in the parking lot outside the Cabin Fever Auction. This old-tool auction is held every February in Nashua, N.H.

Rule #2: Look at what tool collectors don't. One of my best bargains came about because a collector shunned a tool. The owner of a panel-raising plane had restored his tool by refinishing it. The tool looked beautiful to me, but not to a collector. Without its original finish, the plane sold for one-tenth of its value.

Rule #3: Buy parts and pieces. Occasionally, it's a good idea to buy a box lot or two of tool parts because you'll often find a tool with something missing. The tool may be offered cheaply and be in good shape otherwise. To complete the tool, you can simply connect the right part from your stock. My best hand tools have come this way (see the photo at right).

Rule #4: Take it easy. There will always be another tool like the one you want. Don't feel forced into buying a marginal tool or one that costs more than it's worth. It took me nearly three years to put together my assortment of hand tools, and I'm still refining it.

Where to Acquire Old Hand Tools

Vintage tool hunters basically have three avenues where they can buy tools: flea markets, auctions, and dealers. Depending on where you live, the used-tool scene can be quite disorganized and the prices arbitrary. Always remember, it's "buyer beware."

Flea markets offer the best bargains, but they'll cost you energy and time (pleasant work for me). At many flea markets you may only find one tool. But it's likely you'll be able to buy it cheap. My favorite buy was a mint-condition Millers Falls® bit brace—just $3. You can cover a flea market quickly once you learn to spot tool tables from a distance. When you find a tool, don't be afraid to barter. Rarely have I had to pay the marked or asking price.

PUT TOGETHER FOR LESS THAN ONE-FOURTH THE PRICE of a complete plane, this Stanley combination plane is the author's pride and joy. Assembled from parts acquired from flea markets, auctions, and tool dealers, this nonoriginal plane makes a perfectly good woodworking tool, even though it's unacceptable to a collector.

Auctions provide the best selection of tools, but be wary of auction fever. There'll be lots of tools for sale, so wait for a good tool at the right price. To minimize overbidding, first get the auction preview list, even if you have to buy it, and then use preview time wisely (see the top photo on the facing page). Some auctions have previewing the day before, and some require an admittance fee. After I check off items from my want list, I allow five minutes for inspecting each tool. This gives me enough time, even when there's a crowd. If there's no preview list, try to arrive when previewing begins. Do a once over to spot-check all the tools. Then go back and fully inspect items that interest you.

Second, mark down the maximum price you're willing to pay for a tool. I often write the figure on the back of my bidding card along with the lot number (this pre-

**New England Tool Collectors
Association**
164 Chestnut St.
N. Easton, MA 02356-2611

ASSOCIATIONS, AUCTION
HOUSES, AND WORKSHOPS
**Early American Industries
Association**
PO Box 2128, ESP
Albany, NY 12220-0128

**Society of Workers
in Early Arts and Trades**
606 Lake Lena Blvd.
Auburndale, FL 33823

Tool Group of Canada
112 Holmcrest Trail
Scarborough, Ontario
Canada NT M1C 1V5

**The Tool and Trades
Historical Society**
60 Swanley Lane, Swanley, Kent
U.K. BR8 7JG

Your Country Auctioneer Inc.
63 Poor Farm Road,
Hillsboro, NH 03244

National Antique Tool Auction
4729 Kutztown Road
Temple, PA 19560

David Stanley Auctions
Stordon Grange, Osgathorpe
Leicester, U.K. LE12 9SR

ANTIQUE AND USED-TOOL
DEALERS
Tom Witte's Antiques
PO Box 399
Mattawan, MI 49071

**Bob Kaune Antique and Used
Tools**
511 W. 11th St.
Port Angeles, WA 98362

Two Chislers
1864 Glen Moor Drive
Lakewood, CO 80215

Iron Horse Antiques
PO Box 4001
Pittsford, VT 05763

Roger K. Smith
PO Box 177
Athol, MA 01331

Martin Donnelly Antique Tools
31 Rumsey St.
PO Box 281
Bath, NY 14810

BOOKS AND PUBLISHERS
**The Antique Tool Collector's
Guide to Value**
Ronald S. Barlow, 1985,
Windmill Publishing Co.,
2147 Windmill View Road,
El Cajon, CA 92020

The Fine Tool Journal
Iron Horse Antiques,
PO Box 4001
Pittsford, VT 05763

vents me from bidding on a tool that looks identical to the one I want). Once you've arrived at a figure, don't exceed that limit. You'll be strongly tempted to bid another five dollars in hopes of winning a tool, but this rarely works. One exception is when you're bidding against a dealer—they're usually conservative, disciplined bidders. Once they reach their cutoff, you can often buy an item at just a slightly higher bid. On the other end of the spectrum are the collectors. Avoid getting in a bidding war with a collector—they often bid quite aggressively when pursuing tools for their collections.

Third, to save yourself grief, don't bid on something you haven't inspected. I've wound up with lemon tools because I didn't inspect them first. If you can't attend an auction, you may still be able to place a sight-unseen absentee bid, but it is risky. If you're determined to take a risk at an auction, buy a cheap box lot.

Fourth, check out the tailgate tool market, where dealers peddle their wares in event parking lots (see the bottom photo on p. 16).

Dealers have hard-to-find tools, but their prices are frequently higher than those at flea markets and auctions. Many tool dealers sell via mail order and issue some kind of catalog. The catalogs usually list prices and describe tools and their condition. Before you order from a dealer, verify that he has a flexible return policy. Most dealers also have a listing service in which they'll locate something from your want list. Finally, keep an eye open for antique dealers who double as tool dealers.

BOB HUBERT JR. works for an architectural firm. He likes to build period and modern furniture for his Harvard, Massachusetts, home.

Stalking a Secondhand Plane

BY MAURICE FRASER

Acquiring a new handplane can mean spending good time tuning it or else spending dearly for a ready-to-use deluxe model (see the photo below). Another option is to hunt for a usable old classic. So you won't have to hunt in the dark, I'll describe what to watch for when pursuing a used plane, and I'll explore their inner workings.

BASIC PLANE ANATOMY

A plane is, essentially, a chisel locked in a guiding body. Standard bench planes are of three types—each for a special job. The jack plane (14 in. to 15 in. long) zaps wood to dimension, the jointer plane (18 in. to 24 in.) straightens curves, and the smooth plane (8 in. to 9½ in.) polishes surfaces. Except for size, the three types are built alike.

BRITISH AND AMERICAN TRADITIONS

The best metal planes are either the wooden-core British models, exemplified by the classic Norris, or the open-shell cast-iron planes, perfected by the Stanley plane-makers of Connecticut.

Norris and Stanley-type metal planes boast parallel-thicknessed irons, which ensure that the mouth-to-blade fit is constant. In addition, both Norris and Stanley blades have a cap iron bolted to them called, collectively, the "double iron." Both planes lock the double iron to the throat opening with a pivoting lever cap.

Norris-type lever caps are on an axle and tighten to the blade by the turn of a bolt. Stanley-type lever caps are captured under a bolt head and snap tight with a clever cam action: The lever cap consistently forces the blade onto the back of the throat (cutter seat). However, the ideal integral seat isn't feasible in a cast body, so Stanley-types have a screw-on cutter seat or frog, which allows adjustment. Often more a liability than an asset, the frog permits chatter on heavy cuts, and its blade-positioning range can be narrow. Furthermore, Stanley-type frogs wander during adjustment, and realignment is by tedious trial and error. By contrast, the Norris-type cutter seat is simple. It is cut into the solid wood interior and is not adjustable.

INSPIRING SMOOTHERS. The mint-condition used planes in the background (an A-6 Norris, left, and a Stanley No. 4½, right) are hard to find. But, a few new planes borrow features from these originals, as shown in the foreground: Bristol Design's P-40 (left center), J. Warshafsky's 04 Reed (left front), and Record's Calvert-Stevens CS-88 (right front).

CHECKING USED PLANE PARTS: WHAT TO AVOID

A Stanley "Bailey" No. 4
Smooth Plane Assembled

Lever cap has superficial rust.

Cam-actuated locking lever moves hard.

Cap iron edge needs straightening.

Cap iron screw

Slot for depth adjuster

Blade has pitted back.

Slot for lateral adjuster

Reject blade less than ¾ in. left.

Lateral adjustment lever sticks.

Capture bolt for lever cap threads poorly.

Frog

Yoke

Depth adjustment wheel is loose.

Rear tote is cracked.

Front knob has been replaced.

Throat has nick.

Frog setscrews

Patent dates

Frog-adjustment screw is rust-frozen.

Sole of body needs flattening.

Norris-type adjuster

Screw in or out to adjust iron length.

Tilt stern to move iron laterally.

Pivot

Cap receives head of cap-iron screw.

Authentic Norris planes have no frog.

DISASSEMBLY REVEALS PROBLEMS AND VIRTUES. The parts on the left show what to be wary of when buying an old plane. The assembled plane (top right) is fully restored. The Norris-type adjuster (right) is taken from a new Record plane (carried by Garrett Wade).

ADJUSTERS: STANLEY VS. NORRIS

Both Stanley and later Norris metal planes rely on mechanisms to control both depth of cut and side-to-side evenness. Stanley planes separate the two modes of adjustment. For depth, a brass wheel's rotation pushes a forked lever downward, carrying the blade with it. Sideways movement is via a pivoting upright lever, whose end is captive in a blade slot. Norris planes combine the two motions in a single ingenious, but awkward, mechanism (see the inset photo on the facing page).

Stanley's two-part adjustment system is reliable and responsive. Even overused Stanleys adjust with finesse. But a well-preserved Norris adjusts less finely, and it's easy to overtighten the lever cap.

WHAT TO LOOK FOR

Since Norrises are rare and ultraexpensive, start by looking for the upper-end Stanley models: Bailey®, Bedrock®, and Gage. Liberty Bell and Defiance are Stanley's lesser models and may not tune up as well. Most generic "Stanleys" (unsigned) are cheapies and no bargain. Leave exotic brands to the collectors, and as a rule, avoid (or haggle for) planes with mixed parts.

If you're patient and observant, you can avoid buying a plane that will need major work. The photo on the facing page shows a few features that can make or break a deal.

Body:

Normal rust and pitting won't affect a plane's function, but cracks (common around the mouth) are risky and can worsen. Check the sole against a straightedge or a sole of known flatness. If light shows through, the sole will need flattening.

Handles:

Avoid planes without totes. In addition, broken or badly mended totes are like ill-fitting running shoes—no bargain is worth the misery. Note that the totes of long and short planes are not interchangeable. Broken or missing front knobs are replaceable. You can remedy a loose knob or tote by screwing in the retaining bolt or shortening it.

Blades:

Preferably, a blade should be the same make as the plane. A blade ground down to ¾ in. or less from its long slot has little life left (and may have only unhardened steel left in it). Rust pitting on a blade's bevel face is acceptable, but not on the cutting face. The blade's back should be flat and unscored or else proper cap-iron fit will be impossible. Avoid bent blades.

Cap Iron and Lever Cap:

When screwed tight, no light should show at the cap iron's junction with the blade's edge (chips will clog here). If the cap iron is a substitute, its adjuster slot may not align with the depth lever. This limits blade extension, so check out the blade-depth range. A chipped lever cap corner won't affect planing, but the leading contact edge should be straight.

Adjuster and Threaded Parts:

If the brass wheel is rust-frozen, applying WD-40® or oil may or may not free the motion. The yoke should be astride the wheel and freely move with it without rattling. Reject a broken yoke. The lateral adjustment lever can be bent and still function perfectly. Screws should all turn and have reasonably crisp slots and rust-free threads. The lever-cap capture bolt must turn to allow tension adjustment, but rusted frog bolts may never require further use if the frog is set right. If you can, try the tool then and there.

MAURICE FRASER teaches woodworking at the YWCA's Craft Students' League in New York City.

Buying
the Best

BY SCOTT GIBSON

My grandfather's toolbox didn't have much in it besides a hammer, a couple of wrenches, and a spool of baling wire. His small workbench was squeezed in front of the Chevrolet in their cinder block garage. He would have found it hard to believe that anyone not committed to an institution would spend $165 for a jack plane or $50 for a small try square. Plenty of people would agree with him. Even woodworkers who use these tools every day might have trouble swal-

lowing those prices when there are plenty of other tools that supposedly do the same job for a lot less money.

I used to see it that way, too. I figured that the jack plane I already had, a Union No. 5 of unknown age, was fine and that my newest 6-in. square, at about $25, was as accurate as it needed to be. Still, I have long wondered what tools like Lie-Nielsen planes or Bridge City Tool Works® squares and sliding bevels might be like. The ads and catalogs show hand tools of seductive

beauty. I was finally prompted to try some of these tools by something a woodworker said. In preparing to trim a strip of veneer along the edge of a board, he said he reached for his Lie-Nielsen block plane. Not any old block plane, his Lie-Nielsen.

Could it really make that much of a difference? Probably not, I thought, suspecting the comment was really more about tool elitism than anything else. But I wondered enough to get a block plane from Lie-Nielsen and the low-angle jack plane the company also makes. I got my hands on a Bridge City try square, its T1.5 model and borrowed one of its adjustable bevels. Then I set about comparing these tools to the ones that I had been using for years. I wanted to know two things: Were these tools really that much better than what I already had, and would they make any real difference in the quality of my work? I also visited both

of these companies. When paying for pricey tools, I wanted to think I was getting more than a stake in a widget factory. Some of these tools really are worth the price. Others don't look like the right investment for me. It all depends on why you really buy tools—to use, to look at, or some combination of the two.

Where Lie-Nielsens Come From

At Moody's Diner, just a few miles down the road from Lie-Nielsen Toolworks in Warren, Maine, you can still get a cup of coffee for 38 cents, including tax. Pie is extra. Thomas Lie-Nielsen's plane factory, like Moody's Diner, is part of the jumble of motels, snack bars, and gift shops catering to the tourist trade on the road between Wiscasset and Camden. Lie-Nielsen's 6,000-sq.-ft. plant is part machine shop and

THESE PLANES ARE COUSINS, NOT TWINS. A Union No. 5 plane (rear) and a low-angle jack plane from Lie-Nielsen show similarities but big differences, too. The Lie-Nielsen delivers high performance at a high price. The Lie-Nielsen blade (see inset photo) is thicker than the Union's.

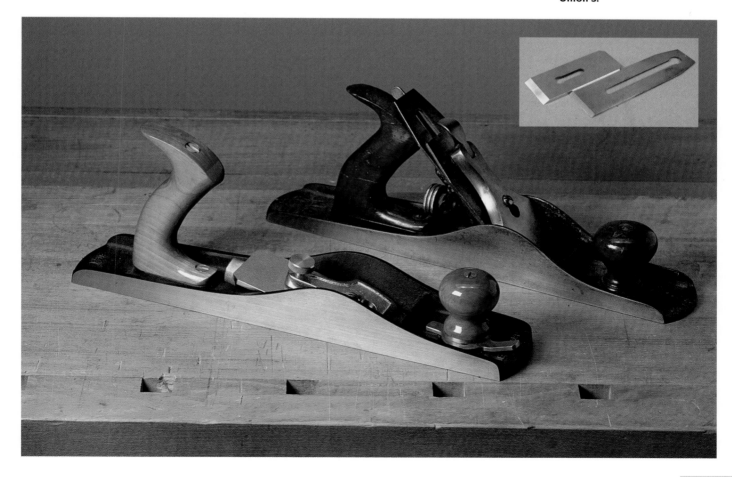

part foundry. Eighteen employees turn out roughly 7,000 planes a year. The first thing you see inside the front door isn't a receptionist's desk. It's a workbench where each of the company's 15 planes is laid out, along with scraps of wood. Visitors are welcome to put a piece of wood in the vise and try any plane that appeals to them.

Lie-Nielsen, 50 and energetic, takes the stairs two at a time. He shares an office with two other employees. He's been making planes for about 24 years, ever since he left his job in 1981 as a tool buyer for Garrett Wade in New York City. When a supplier told Garrett Wade that it would stop making its edge-trimming block plane, Lie-Nielsen saw an opportunity to go back to Maine and become a plane maker.

He had no formal training as a machinist or foundry worker. But he set himself up in a West Rockport woodshed (not fancy enough to be called a workshop, he says) and began figuring out how to make the plane. It was complicated. The first castings were done by a friend nearby. In six months, Lie-Nielsen delivered 100 planes to Garrett Wade. He slowly taught himself the skills he needed, and the business grew from there.

Almost all of his planes are modeled after ones the rest of the world stopped making many years ago: a skew block plane similar to a Stanley No. 140, No. 1, and No. 2 smooth planes, a 10-in.-long chisel plane, a scraping plane. Most of the planes have bodies made of manganese bronze. Later this year, he hopes to introduce a No. 4 smooth plane, a standard-size bench plane. That would put him head-to-head against a number of other mainstream manufacturers.

Everything in a Lie-Nielsen plane, with the exception of the cast-iron bodies on four models, is made in the Warren plant: adjusting screws, irons, cherry handles (see the photo at right). Lie-Nielsen is trying to

cross-train employees to reduce the company's reliance on his own production know-how. But there are still operations, like hardening plane irons in a liquid salt bath, that he hasn't given up. Quality control is rigid. There are no Lie-Nielsen seconds —what can't be sold is melted down for another try.

Okay, but How Do They Work?

I doubt there's a tool in my shop I use more often than my Record low-angle block plane. It's sweet. The jack plane I own does what the block plane won't. Because of its length, a jack plane spans greater distances than a block plane and is an all-around heavier tool. Taken together, there aren't a lot of planing jobs these two won't do.

The Lie-Nielsen block plane is a little smaller than my Record, so it fits in my hand more comfortably (see the photo

PRODUCTION RUNS ARE VERY SMALL. Molten manganese bronze is poured into sand molds at Lie-Nielsen Toolworks to form plane bodies.

below). Mechanically, the two planes are similar but not identical. The Record has an adjustable throat, which the Lie-Nielsen lacks, and the cap irons differ slightly in how they work. One real difference is the blades, on the jack plane as well as the block plane. The Lie-Nielsen blades are thicker and seem to hold an edge longer. The difference in cost—$75 for the Lie-Nielsen and about $50 for the Record— would make it easy to buy the Lie-Nielsen if I had the choice to make over again.

There are far more differences between the two jack planes, as shown in the photo on p. 23. The blade in the Union No. 5 (a typical metal-bodied bench plane like a Stanley or a Record) is set at 45 degrees and goes in bevel side down with a lever cap to keep it in place. There's a lateral adjustment to square the blade in the throat.

The Lie-Nielsen jack plane is a different animal. Its blade is set at 12 degrees to the sole, bevel up, with no chipbreaker. There is no lateral adjustment (the blade is precisely milled to fit in the body of the plane), and the throat opening is adjustable. This jack plane is based on the Stanley No. 62, which was used to smooth the end grain of butcher blocks.

Hard, curly maple is just about the most ornery wood I know. I've never had a lot of luck planing this stuff by hand with either a block plane or a jack plane. The undulating figure makes for easy tearout and chipping just where you don't want it. I've always found it easier to get the dimensions close to where they want to be and then sand. And sand. That was until I unboxed the Lie-Nielsen plane and ran it down a 1½-in.- wide piece of curly with an especially heavy wave. I got paper-thin shavings, not chunks of wood. And the plane left behind a surface that was ready for finish: glassy smooth, almost polished (see the photo on p. 26). This is how planing should be. You want to plane for no other reason than the feel of the tool slicing through the wood.

The Union plane, even after a good sharpening, just couldn't match that performance. Although the surface of the planed wood was relatively smooth, there were those telltale peck-outs that I've come to associate with hand tools on curly maple. Close, but no cigar. The comparable results were essentially the same on cherry and pine.

I wanted to hate this tool. I liked to think of it as a trophy for tool junkies. But I didn't have the Lie-Nielsen in my hands for more than five minutes before I wanted to buy it. At $165, it isn't cheap. But for anyone working difficult woods by hand, this plane is easily worth the cost.

Bridge City Tool Works

Company founder John Economaki eventually would like to make every tool a woodworker needs that doesn't have a power cord attached to it. For now, Bridge City makes layout tools—straightedges, marking gauges, squares, trammels, and adjustable bevels. His company sells somewhere between 30,000 and 50,000 tools a year. His product line has doubled in the last three years, and he plans to introduce five new tools a year for the foreseeable future.

THE LIE-NIELSEN IS SMALLER. Its low-angle block plane (left) is smaller than a Record and contoured for a more comfortable fit.

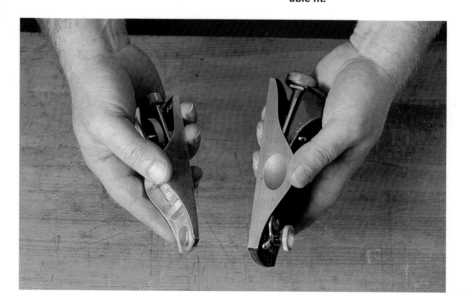

He now runs three shifts at his Portland, Ore., plant and still can't keep up with demand. Just about everything he sells is back ordered; you could wait as long as nine months for some of the 42 tools in his catalog. After several financially punishing years in the early '90s, Economaki wants to take his company public this year by selling up to 400,000 shares of common stock.

Economaki is a 43-year-old former shop teacher from Iowa who moved to Portland in 1973 for his first teaching job. A video and, later, a workshop by furniture maker Sam Maloof changed his life. After teaching for six years, he turned pro as a furniture maker. Then, in 1982, a severe allergy to wood dust made it hard to continue working in the shop. So he turned to toolmaking. He started with a scratch awl and a square that he had originally designed as a project for his ninth-grade shop class (the ones he bought for the class were all out of square).

Economaki thinks cheap tools are a waste of natural resources. He believes that the quality of American hand tools dropped like a stone after World War II when American factories rushed to supply the rest of the planet with manufactured goods. "It was all sort of adequate," he says with a shrug.

His company's motto is "quality is contagious." To Economaki, that means the overall quality of his tools should encourage woodworkers who use them to do their best work. The excellence of a Bridge City square, for instance, just leads to better work. And, he says, his squares are dead-on accurate. To Economaki, it's all about value: "If you're serious about woodworking, you should be buying serious tools."

The squares, marking gauges, and other tools are built in 13,300 sq. ft. of second-floor space in a 1902 wood-frame factory that's anything but pretentious. Computer-controlled milling machines do the heavy work, but each tool makes the rounds of workbenches where assembly, fitting, and polishing are done by hand (see the photo on p. 29). Bridge City does sell seconds, but only if the imperfections are cosmetic. I like Bridge City tools for the way they work and for the way they look, but I'd have a hard time spending the money for most of them. The reason? To me, the difference between an accurate but moderately priced tool and a much more expensive version from Bridge City seems largely cosmetic. But they are nice.

High Performance at a High Cost

The Bridge City TS 1.5 try square is similar in size to a Sorby square I bought a few years ago for about $25. At the time I thought the Sorby was quite an extravagance. According to the Bridge City catalog, the TS 1.5 is just right for making boxes or drawers. Accuracy is guaranteed to within .002 in. over the length of the blade. It's beautifully made, with a thick brass blade and a dark wooden handle.

The handle material on Bridge City tools, as it turns out, is something of a sore point among some Bridge City fans. Some of them complain that handles are no longer made of rosewood. Economaki stopped using rosewood in his regular production-run tools three or four years ago (some new tool releases still get it) for a variety of reasons. The substitute is called Juara wood, as if it were some kind of wood species. It is, sort of. As the catalog explains, Juara is really strips of maple, birch, or beech laminated together and impregnated with phenolic resin and dyed to a pleasant, rosewood-like color. The stuff is probably indestructible, and Economaki pays twice as much for it as he does for rosewood. It sure doesn't offend me.

Well, what does a square do, anyway? It lays out a line square to an edge, or it's used to check that two surfaces are square to each other. As far as that goes, the Bridge City square and the Sorby square both do the same job. Both seem to do it accurately.

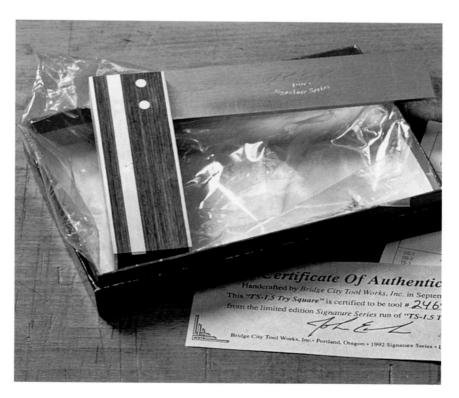

CAREFUL PACKAGING, GUARANTEED ACCURACY. The Bridge City try square is made of heavy brass and a laminated wooden handle. It comes with a certificate of accuracy.

ADJUSTABLE SLIDING BEVELS IN THREE GRADES. The Bridge City bevel (bottom) is built to last, with a price tag to match. The other two are from Stanley, one old (top) and the other recent.

The Bridge City square is more comfortable to hold because the handle isn't as wide as the one on the Sorby. And it's certainly better looking. But as far as I can tell, there's no difference in useful accuracy between the two. I can't claim my four-year-old Sorby is within .002 in. (which means the blade won't be out more than $\frac{1}{500}$ in. over its length). But when I draw parallel lines on a board with both the Sorby and the Bridge City squares to test accuracy, the results look the same to me.

I'm not going to lose much sleep if my own square is a couple thousandths of an inch off. That level of accuracy seems beside the point when I'm working on something like a tenon for a door rail, especially in a nice softwood like pine. Neither my handsaw nor my tablesaw will cut a line that accurately. And gluing up the door frame in clamps would take out .002 in. of slop. It's a different story when using a square to

check that sawblades or jointer fences are set accurately. In that case, I want to know the square I'm using is right on. Even so, I didn't end up feeling that I had to own a Bridge City square. As handsome and accurate as it is, I get the same performance and nearly the same aesthetics from a tool that costs roughly half as much. For me, the Bridge City square isn't a good buy.

Bridge City Adjustable Bevel

There may be a better case for buying Bridge City's 7-in. adjustable sliding bevel. A friend of mine loaned me his (he told me twice to be careful with it) and said he'd never had anything that held an angle as well. Like most Bridge City tools, this one is made with heavy brass-wear plates and has a solid, reliable sort of heft. I have several sliding bevels but none as pretty as this tool (see the photo above).

The bevel I use most of the time is a very old Stanley, with what looks like a walnut handle and a brass lever that tightens the blade. It's beat up, but I can set an angle one-handed, which I can't with the Bridge City tool. I paid a couple of bucks for it at a barn sale and wouldn't trade it for a Bridge City bevel if only because I've had it for a long time.

A newer and smaller Stanley bevel that I also own would be a much better reason to consider a Bridge City bevel. Even though the difference in price is big (the Bridge City is $69), the Stanley frustrates me every time I pick it up. It has an uninspiring wooden handle, and the wing nut that tightens the blade is uncomfortable to use and interferes with the work. It would be worth the $69 not to have to use it again. So if I were starting from scratch and didn't have a sliding bevel, I'd consider the Bridge City tool. But not now. I'm left with the feeling that there are less-expensive alternatives for bevels that perform just as well.

Not everyone, of course, buys tools for purely practical reasons. I don't either, really. Tools can be appealing just because they feel right in your hand or because they're plain beautiful. I've bought tools for those reasons, and I hope I do again. And Economaki may have something when he says the quality of a person's tools will be reflected in his work. Aesthetics alone, though, usually aren't enough for me. If I'm going to spend a lot of money for a tool, I want it to earn its keep with the work it does, not necessarily with the way it looks. If money were no object, I'd enjoy working with nothing but top-drawer hand tools, no matter what task they performed. Life being what it is, I can make do without some of them.

SCOTT GIBSON is a freelance writer and editor living in Maine. He is the author of *The Workshop* (Taunton Press, 2003).

TOOLS ARE MADE ONE STEP AT A TIME. Modern milling machines at Bridge City take care of the heavy work, but tools spend more time making the rounds in small batches for hand fitting and polishing.

Four-Squaring with Hand Tools

BY ANTHONY GUIDICE

In my woodworking classes, before I let students use machines, they are required to rip, crosscut, surface, and edge-joint boards—a process called four-squaring—by hand. Hand-tool methods bring students closer to the process. They can understand wood easier—grain characteristics and vagaries—when they work it by hand. Hand tools make wood more of a sensitive material you pay attention to, not some impersonal matrix you ram through a machine. Plus, hand-tool work will stand you in good stead some day if one of your machines is down and you can't get parts for a week.

Most problems students have with hand tools stem from using lousy, dull tools. You can't do serious work with grandpa's old, rusty plane, and even lots of new tools aren't very good. I use a five-point German bowsaw for dimensioning. It cuts fast and accurately. I use Lie-Nielsen planes. Sharpen them, and they cut beautifully right off the shelf. No other metal planes do. These planes have solid castings, thick blades made of good steel and are manufactured to close tolerances. Nothing is more infuriating than trying to do sustained, serious work with a plane that has a wavy sole and a tinny blade that won't stay sharp or with a clumsy saw that has too thick a blade and an uncomfortable handle.

Good tools will solve 90% of problems in hand-tool use. Keeping them razor sharp will solve another 5%. Most students think they are at fault as they try to chip and bang their way through a board. Then they try my tools and discover their cheap planes and saws were the culprits—not them. The last 5% of hand-tool problems can be alleviated with practice. Think of how awkward you felt the first time you drove a car.

The Beauty of the Bowsaw

Start the four-squaring process by using a sharp pencil or a razor knife to mark a line across a board, then crosscut the board to a rough length. (You'll cut the board to final

CROSSCUT WITH A BOWSAW. **Keep your wrist angled outward, and with a little practice, you'll be able to make square cuts.**

length as the last step.) Lop off the first 4 in. or so of the board to remove end-grain cracks.

When you first start using a handsaw, the tendency is to angle the blade in toward you. The same thing can happen when you hand-cut bread. But if you make an effort to angle your wrist outward and away from you, cutting squarely will be much easier. It's just a matter of practice—like hitting a tin can with a BB gun.

If it seems daunting to cut accurately in two planes at once—the face and the edge—you may be using the wrong saw. A bowsaw has a thin, 1⅜-in.-wide blade that is held in tension in the frame. It cuts very quickly, won't whip or kink in the kerf, and is easy to control. You can cut to a line—an essential skill—easily with a bowsaw. Small wonder the bowsaw is a staple tool in Europe. I don't know why we haven't heard more about this tool in the United States.

Flatten with a Scrub Plane

The scrub plane is the most crucial plane in the mix, yet it is the most overlooked and misunderstood. A scrub plane flattens a board; that is, it takes out the twist, warp, and bow. A jack plane can remove high spots left by the scrub plane, but you can't

flatten a board with one. A jointer plane can square an edge and remove the last high spots from the face, but it can't flatten a board, either. A board can be flattened only with a scrub plane.

Lots of woodworking students think they can use a jack plane to do the work of a scrub plane. Forget it. It won't work. To flatten wood you need to remove unwanted areas in big pieces. If you try it with a jack plane, you'll end up with a smoothly sur-faced, unflat board. It's like giving coffee to an inebriated person—you'll get a wide-awake drunk. The intentions are good, but the result is bad.

Scrub planes are designed to do one thing: flatten wood. The scrub-plane blade is radiused—it scoops like a gouge. It doesn't shave like a regular plane. Most problems arise from trying to take too big a cut with it. I regrind my Lie-Nielsen scrub-plane blade to a 2¼-in. radius, then sharpen and polish it with waterstones.

Clamp the board on the bench. With about ¹⁄₁₆ in. to ⅛ in. of the blade showing, plane the board diagonally all the way in one direction, then the other. If the board has any pronounced bulges or high ends, plane those spots more. Flip over the board, and with your fingers on opposite corners, try to rock the board on the bench. Try one pair of corners, then the other. If the board rocks, there is a high spot. It's easy to find by bringing your fingers in from the corners toward the middle of the board while continuing to rock it. When the board stops rocking, the high spot is between your hands. Flip the board over again and remove the high spot with a scrub plane.

Plane the High Spots

Next, jack-plane the high spots—the crest of the waves left by the scrub plane. I use a No. 5 jack plane, about 14 in. long and set for a heavy cut—it will take off a big piece. If the cut is too light, this step will seem to take forever. My jack plane has an adjustable throat, so I open that up a little, too. Work the plane on the board the same way: diagonally, first in one direction, then the other.

Use more pressure on the front handle to start the cut, equal pressure front and back in the middle, and more pressure on the rear tote as you finish. This technique

JOINTER PLANE IS THE LAST ONE TO USE. **With a long jointer plane, work the board with the grain, removing the marks left by the jack plane.**

will keep you from rounding down the edges. If that happens, the board will rock again when you flip it over, and you'll have to start over.

After taking off the high spots with the jack plane diagonally, plane with the grain using the jointer plane. If you use a good jointer plane, it will take up long, thin shavings easily (a lousy, dull one will skip and jump). Because grain always seems to change direction in the middle of a board, you may get some tearout. But tearout isn't all bad—you are doing handwork; the piece should look handmade, not manufactured. After using the jointer plane, flip over the board again and make sure it doesn't rock. No need to be fanatical; you're working wood, not uranium. If it doesn't rock noticeably, it's good. That side is done.

Set a marking gauge for the final desired thickness. Bearing the fence on the face you've just done, mark a line all the way around the board. Clamp the board in the bench with the now-flat side down, and plane to the mark, working in sequence as before. Work the scrub plane to a little less than 1/16 in. of the line. The jack and jointer planes will get you to it.

Joint One Edge

With the faces of the board surfaced, plane one edge flat and square to the faces with the jointer plane. Clamp the board sideways in the bench. Take long passes with the jointer plane until the edge is straight and square.

Hold the jointer plane by the front handle and the rear tote, and guide it over the edge 90 degrees to the face by eye. With a little practice, you'll also be able to see and feel a 90 degrees cut here. Check it with a square from time to time, but don't use jigs, a fence, or any other nonsense. And don't hold the plane so that you can guide it with your fingers underneath. Hold the plane by the handles. Your eye-hand coordination is

MARKING GAUGE DETERMINES THICKNESS. After one face of the board has been planed flat and smooth, run a marking-gauge fence along the finished side to mark the board's final thickness. Repeat the three-plane process on the rough, unfinished side.

BOWSAW FOR RIPPING TO FINAL WIDTH. The saw's long blade makes it easy to take long strokes. Cut to within 1/16 in. of the marked line. Finish the sawn edge with a jointer plane.

USE A STRAIGHTEDGE TO MARK A PARALLEL EDGE. Hold a pencil against the blade of a combination square set to the desired width and mark a line on the opposite side.

better than any gimmick or trick grip. Learn the correct way once, and you'll always know.

Rip the Opposite Side

With one edge straight, the next step is to make the opposite edge straight and parallel to it. Use a combination square and pencil to draw a continuous line for a rip cut with the bowsaw. Clamp the board in the bench horizontally, with the edge to be cut hang-

ing off the side. Turn the bowsaw blade askew to the frame and saw down the line. Keep the blade cutting just outside the line—about 1/32 in.—then plane it to the line afterward. The large teeth and long blade of the bowsaw make this fast work. When the board has been ripped to width, clamp up the newly sawn edge in the bench and plane to the edge using a jointer plane. The last step is to use the bowsaw again, this time to square up the ends of the nice, flat board with the parallel sides.

Using hand tools to do this kind of work is important, not so much because it makes the wood different but because it makes the woodworker different. You'll gain an acuity and respect for wood that you cannot get by being a machine operator. When you can dimension a board flat and square by hand, you'll have achieved something that only a small percentage of woodworkers can do or will even bother to attempt. You'll be a different woodworker, too. A better one.

ANTHONY GUIDICE builds custom furniture and teaches woodworking in St. Louis, Missouri.

Bench-Chisel Techniques

BY GARRETT HACK

A few thousand years ago, someone clever hammered out a hunk of bronze into a narrow blade, fitted a handle to one end, sharpened the other against a stone, and produced a chisel. Generations of craftsmen since have tweaked the design: Tough steel replaced soft bronze, the shape and length of the blade were modified to suit various tasks, but in essence, chisels have not changed much. They are still simple in form and, when used effectively, one of the most useful tools in the shop.

Every week catalogs arrive, full of a dizzying array of different chisels: long, fine-bladed paring chisels; stout mortise chisels; heavy and wide framing chisels; stubby butt chisels; intriguing Japanese chisels; and many sets of bench chisels. Few other classic hand tools are still available in such variety. Unless you work entirely by hand, all you really need is a good set of what I call bench chisels or, as some prefer, firmer chisels. These are chisels with blades about 4 in. to 6 in. long, in a wide range of widths from about $\frac{1}{8}$ in. to 2 in. and with a wooden or plastic handle.

The only substantial differences between sets of bench chisels are the quality of the

The Most Versatile Tool in Your Shop

No bench is complete without a chisel. Generations of woodworkers have come up with multiple uses for the chisel far beyond its original purpose. The five photos to the right show a chisel replacing tweezers, a hollow-chisel mortiser, a pencil sharpener, a scraper, and a handplane.

BETTER THAN TWEEZERS. Perhaps best not done in front of children, removing a splinter with a chisel works faster than tweezers.

SQUARING UP MORTISES. When squaring up a machine-made mortise, a block of wood clamped to the workpiece can act as a guide.

HANDY PENCIL SHARPENER. A test of a chisel's edge is how fine a point you can put on a pencil.

CLEAN UP GLUE SQUEEZE-OUT. A scraper works best for large areas, but for small areas a chisel offers more control.

PARING PEGS. A chisel with a flat back offers more control than a plane and is neater than a sander when leveling a pin.

steel and the shapes of the blades. The blades on my everyday set of Swedish bench chisels are slightly tapered in length and beveled along the long sides. Tapering the blade yields a tool stout enough for the hard work of chopping a mortise yet light enough to pare one-handed. A blade with flat sides is stronger than one with beveled sides and is less expensive to manufacture. But a beveled blade can reach into tighter places, such as for cutting small dovetails.

Prepare the Chisel

As with many other tools, the performance of a chisel is determined by how well it is tuned. The back of the chisel—the unbeveled side—must be dead flat for at least ¾ in., and preferably 1 in. to 2 in., behind the cutting edge. This flat plane guides and controls the cut: A curved back will rock and provide little control.

Honing a Chisel

FIRST FLATTEN THE TOOL'S BACK. At least the first ¾ in., and preferably the first 1 in. to 2 in., of the chisel's back should be perfectly flat. The back guides and controls the cut and ensures a fine edge.

GRIND AND HONE. After hollow-grinding a 25° bevel on the grinder, the author hones the bevel on a medium and then a fine oilstone. The author guides the chisel free-hand, but a honing guide can help until you master the technique.

READY TO CUT. The tuned chisel should be flat on the back and have a narrow band of honed steel along the cutting edge, with a slightly concave ground surface just behind. If you can leave a clean cut on pine end grain, your chisel is ready for action.

Another common problem is a slight rounding of the cutting edge on the back side. The back might still be flat except for this tiny back-bevel. Sloppy technique, not keeping the back absolutely flat on a sharpening stone while honing, creates this sort of rounding. The result is a chisel that will not cut while resting on its back because the rounded edge is in the air. A chisel with a rounded edge must be angled forward slightly, thus losing the back as a source of control. Flattening the back of a bench chisel right to the cutting edge is tedious but important. Work through the range of grits until you get a bright polish on your finest stone.

Once you have flattened the back, choose a cutting bevel angle based on the type of work you do. The finer the bevel, the more easily the tool slices through wood fibers. A fine bevel, 15 degrees to 20 degrees, is a little delicate, but it works for a chisel reserved for light paring cuts in softwoods. To chop tough end grain, a stouter 30- to 35-degree bevel would hold up better. For everyday bench work I aim for a 25-degree bevel whose width is about twice the thickness of the chisel. This is a compromise between ease of cutting and the durability of the edge.

Lightly hollow-grinding the bevel every three to four sharpenings speeds the honing process by reducing the area of steel in contact with the stone. I use a grooved block of wood that holds the chisel handle, set at a distance from the wheel to achieve the desired bevel angle. I then hone the edge on a medium India stone and a fine black Arkansas stone using kerosene as a lubricant. I try to hone at a consistent 25-degree bevel with little or no microbevel along the cutting edge. The only exception is when I need a slightly tougher cutting edge for an extremely hard wood, such as rosewood, where I raise the tool handle to hone a microbevel of 30 degrees. For a final strop I use some 0- to 2-micron diamond paste smeared on a piece of Baltic birch plywood. I prefer this to a leather strop, which being softer and more uneven increases the risk of rounding over the bevel.

How to Tell if Your Chisel Is Sharp

It's worth repeating that a chisel must be very sharp to work well. A dull edge takes far more power to drive through the fibers and, more important, is harder to control. Everyone has a special way to test the sharpness of an edge: dragging it against a fingernail, shaving arm hair, or plucking the edge with a finger. The problem is that these tests are all a bit subjective.

I test the sharpness of a chisel by paring a block of end-grain white pine and then looking at both the shaving and the cut surface. Because softwood fibers are weak and easily torn from the surface, only a really sharp edge will cut a thin and whole shaving. Looking at the end grain; ideally it should be uniformly polished. But more likely there will be light flecks in the surface where fibers were torn away, or it will exhibit fine tracks where tiny nicks in the chisel's cutting edge scraped across the wood.

Next lay the chisel with the back flat on one of the long-grain sides of your block. If you can pare a shaving without lifting the chisel, the back and cutting edge are flat. If you have to lift the chisel to get it to cut, the back or cutting edge is rounded.

Proper Technique Ensures Good Results

For most of us, the days of working with hand tools alone are long gone. Whereas chisels would once have been our primary tools for cutting all manner of joints, today we typically use them more often to adjust joints cut on a machine.

Chiseling tasks can be simplified to chopping, paring, or some combination of

Vertical Chopping and Paring

With experience you will be able to hold the chisel at the correct angle merely by sighting across and down it (right). A square set on end acts as a guide when squaring up the end of a mortise (below right).

Lighten up as you near your mark. Particularly in softwood, chopping too much waste at once makes the bevel push the chisel back over the line (top photo, below). It is better to take small cuts (bottom photo, below) and sneak up to the line.

the two. Cutting end grain, such as excavating a mortise, is chopping. A mallet usually delivers the driving force, so everything works best when you chop vertically, down against your bench, preferably directly over a leg. Paring is often a hand-powered operation, using the chisel horizontally or vertically to slice away a thin shaving. This can be against the end grain or along the grain.

CHOP, THEN PARE. Lightly chopping all the way around defines the shoulder of a tenon (left) before a final paring with hand power (above).

line. Try to chop too large a chip, especially in softwood, and the pressure will push your chisel beyond your line. Take little bites, waste up to your line, and then take a final light cut right on the line. Because I have a good selection of chisel sizes, I waste as much wood as I can with a chisel narrower than the mortise. The final cut is with a chisel snug in the mortise and right on the line.

Paring to a line vertically Paring end grain gives you a whole new appreciation for the toughness of wood. Good paring takes both muscle and a feel for controlling the cut. A sharp chisel and a light cut give you the best chance for doing accurate work.

I also pare with the chisel in one hand and use my thumb as a lever, much the same way you would use a knife.

Chopping to a line vertically Cutting with a chisel held plumb is an acquired skill. Finding the right angle is easiest when you are only slightly above the work and looking across the chisel. Sighting against a square set on end helps, as does good light shining toward the work and you. Holding the chisel plumb greatly speeds any chopping task. If this is hard for you, or if you have to cut an angled mortise, saw a waste block to this angle and clamp it in place to guide your chisel. For heavy chopping, driving a chisel with a mallet allows you to concentrate all of your efforts on directing the tool.

Light cuts yield more accurate results. Think about the cutting edge sinking into the wood. The back is trying to guide the chisel plumb while the beveled side of the cutting edge presses the chisel against the back. With a light cut this pressure breaks out the chip and holds the back right to the

Horizontal Paring

When cutting horizontally, the smoothest cuts are made with a slight shearing action, cutting both forward and sideways. The need for a perfectly flat chisel back is apparent when fitting a tenon.

After you have removed the bulk of the waste using a mallet, switch to a light paring cut right on the line. This provides greater accuracy and control and allows you to undercut slightly. Also, it's just plain quicker than reaching for the mallet each time after moving the work. Work around all four sides of a tenon to establish the shoulder line and to give you something to sight against when paring. Position your body above the work for paring the final shaving or two, using the weight of your upper body to drive the chisel and both hands to guide it.

Paring to a line horizontally Given a choice, I prefer the control of a plane to shave a surface. But there are plenty of times when I don't have the right plane close at hand or when it's simply quicker to pare a few shavings with a chisel. Long and thin-bladed (for flexibility) paring chisels are the tools of choice here, but a well-tuned bench chisel will work almost as well.

For maximum control when paring, I find it's best to have one hand on the chisel handle and the other as close to the work, or cutting edge, as practical. This way you can raise or lower the handle slightly to control the depth of cut, while the hand close to the cutting edge holds the chisel steady and helps guide the cut. This hand also acts as a brake, smoothing out the pressure delivered by the hand on the handle. The smoothest and easiest cuts are made with a slight shearing action, slicing both forward and sideways.

Paring while using the thumb as a lever Holding the chisel like a penknife or a potato peeler, with the blade cutting toward you, takes some getting used to. Once mastered, this technique allows for fine controlled cuts, even in end grain. I use it to pare the end of a table leg, to shorten a tenon, and to chamfer its ends.

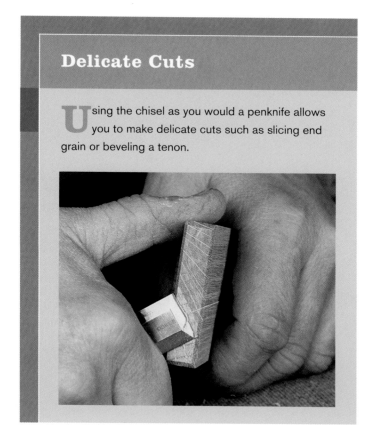

Delicate Cuts

Using the chisel as you would a penknife allows you to make delicate cuts such as slicing end grain or beveling a tenon.

Cutting bevel-side down When paring the bottom of a groove, the flat back of a chisel can no longer be used as a guide and the natural inclination of the chisel is to dig in. Turn the chisel upside down and use the bevel to guide the cut, raising or lowering the handle to adjust the depth of the cut. This method is useful to deepen a mortise or dado (or shape a curved one) or to smooth the bottom of a recess for an inlay.

As with all tools, there are many paths to accurate and satisfying results. Sharpen a few chisels and practice these basic techniques. Some of them might not feel comfortable at first, but everyday use at your bench is the surest way to master them.

GARRETT HACK is a furniture maker in Thetford Center, Vermont.

Backsaw Workshop

BY PHILIP C. LOWE

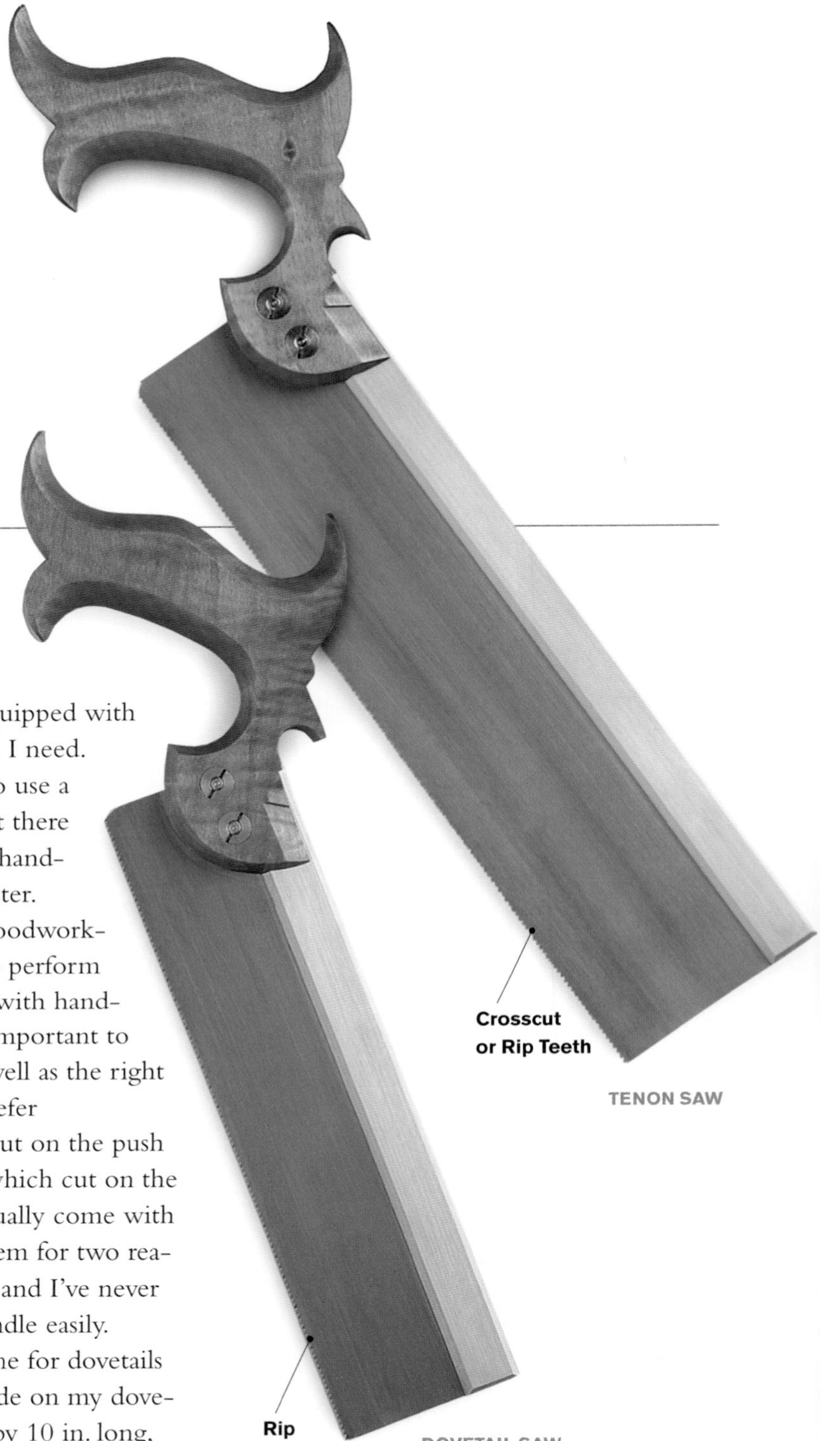

My shop is fully equipped with every power tool I need. I don't hesitate to use a power tool to save time. But there are occasions when using a handsaw is more efficient and faster. Handsaws often frustrate woodworkers who cannot get them to perform well. After 35 years cutting with handsaws, I've found that it's as important to use the right technique as well as the right saw to get good results. I prefer Western-style saws, which cut on the push stroke, over Japanese saws, which cut on the pull stroke. Western saws usually come with a pistol grip, and I prefer them for two reasons: I was trained on them and I've never met a task they couldn't handle easily.

I have three backsaws: one for dovetails and two for tenons. The blade on my dovetail saw is about 2 in. wide by 10 in. long, with 15 tpi, and is sharpened for rip cuts because dovetails are cut with or along the grain. The set of the teeth is minimal, so the kerf is not too wide.

As for my tenon saws, one is sharpened for rip cuts (the cheeks of a tenon), and the other for crosscuts (across the grain at the shoulders). Each saw has a 15-tpi blade that's 3 in. wide and 14 in. long. The wider

Crosscut or Rip Teeth

TENON SAW

Rip Teeth

DOVETAIL SAW

TYPES OF BACKSAWS. The "back" in backsaw refers to the reinforcing strip along the saw's spine. But backsaws vary in shape and size and come with different tooth patterns. Dovetail saws are smaller and are sharpened for rip cuts. Larger tenon saws come with tooth patterns for either ripping or crosscutting. If you decide to buy only one tenon saw, choose one with crosscut teeth.

blade allows for cutting tenons of substantial length.

Though I depend on all three saws, if I had to buy only one, it would be a dovetail saw. Its blade is wide enough to cut most tenons, and the teeth are so fine that it will cut cross-grain well enough.

Begin with a Proper Grip and Stance

The manner in which you grip the saw is critical. When holding a pistol-grip saw, keep your wrist straight and point your index finger toward the blade. This keeps the saw from twisting in your hand and directs the cut. Don't choke the handle; rather, hold it as if you were holding a bird and didn't want it to get away.

Stance is also key to achieving an even, smooth action for cutting. When addressing your work, your arm and shoulder should be aligned with the cut. If you crowd the work, your elbow is forced away from your body to avoid hitting your side. You then make a sideward movement and your hand travels in an arc. If you are standing in the correct position, your shoulder, elbow and wrist are in a straight line and all pivot from the shoulder. Your feet should be positioned so that the one that is opposite your cutting arm is forward and the other behind. This allows for your back foot and arm to take any resistance that is exerted from the saw and prevents you from being knocked off balance.

Keep your eyes on the cut line during the whole cut to ensure that the kerf doesn't stray from the line. For dovetail cuts, look at the top line across the width of the board and the line down the face of the board to make sure you're cutting in a straight line.

Rips and Crosscuts Require Different Techniques

The method for beginning a cut with a backsaw depends on whether you're ripping or crosscutting. When making a rip

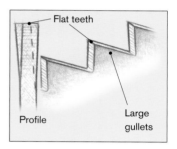

Ripsaw teeth
The flat-top teeth act as chisels and are designed to cut with the grain. They are spaced farther apart (from 12 tpi to 20 tpi), and the gullets are deeper to clear out sawdust as you cut.

Flat teeth

Profile

Large gullets

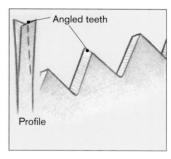

Crosscut teeth
The angled teeth score the cross-grain fibers as they cut. The teeth are smaller and cut slower than ripsaw teeth.

Angled teeth

Profile

cut for a tenon or a dovetail, place your thumbnail on the pencil or scribe mark and rest the saw against your nail. Push the saw forward with a light stroke, then follow the line as best as possible. When crosscutting, align your index, middle, and ring fingers along the scribe line. When using a crosscut tenon saw, start the cut with a light push stroke. Slight pressure against your fingers prevents the saw from drifting into the scribe line.

Grip and Stance

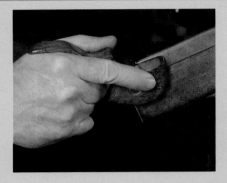

POINT YOUR INDEX FINGER toward the workpiece (left) to keep the saw straight. Keep your knees bent and your arm low and angled up toward the workpiece (below).

Remember that these saws cut only on the push stroke. Some people try to start a cut by making a small kerf with a pull, or draw, stroke of the saw. But if pressure is exerted on the pull stroke you will experience excessive vibration, often even more apparent with a coarse-toothed blade. If starting the cut on the push stroke is difficult, it's probably time to get your saw sharpened. I've found that even a new saw needs to be sharpened before it can be used. You can sharpen the blade yourself, but it may be worthwhile to find a local shop that will sharpen the saw to your specifications. Also, Woodcraft® offers a sharpening service (see Sources).

A slow, smooth, even stroke with constant pressure is what you are after. On the push stroke, be sure to use the full length of the blade and avoid short strokes. On the pull stroke, ease the pressure to prevent vibration. When cutting tenons or dovetails, start your cuts at the corner of the board and follow the line down and across the top until you reach the scribe lines or the opposite side of the piece. At this point, if you are cutting a tenon, continue by following the kerf down the back line. It is only necessary to watch the opposite side if you are approaching a scribe line that you don't want to cut beyond. But in most cases you ought to make the shoulder cuts first.

Workpiece Position Should Simplify Cutting

When cutting dovetails, hold your work vertically in a vise. When cutting the tails, I like to tip the board so that the angle is vertical and the saw does not have to be tipped. I think it's easier to teach your body to cut a straight line that is perpendicular to your bench than to cut at an angle.

Clamp tenon stock in a vise so that you cut from the front of the vise. Ideally, the part should be positioned so that the rip

Sawing Dovetails

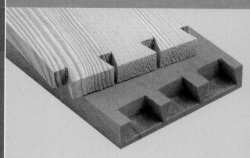

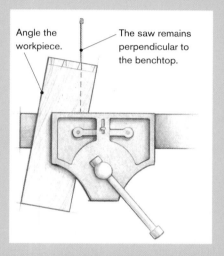

Angle the workpiece.

The saw remains perpendicular to the benchtop.

ANGLE THE WORK, not the saw, when cutting tails. It's easier to cut a straight line if you're cutting perpendicular to the bench.

An upward cut slices cleanly through the long grain.

HOLD THE WORK VERTICALLY when cutting pins. Use your thumbnail as a guide and begin the cut on the push stroke.

CROSSCUT THE SHOULDERS. **Use a bench hook to hold the work. Using your fingertips to guide the saw (above), start on the push stroke at a very slight angle and then level out to complete the cut.**

cuts proceed vertically. This is not always possible when cutting tenons that have compound angles. When crosscutting shoulders on tenons, hold the part in a vise or with a bench hook.

Most Cutting Problems Have Simple Solutions

If you are having trouble making straight, clean cuts, there are a few things to look out for. If your saw binds, check the blade.

New saws have lacquer on the sides of the blade that can soften from friction and make the saw grab. Remove the lacquer with lacquer thinner and apply a coat of paste wax to the metal sides. Rust can also cause binding. Remove it with silicon-carbide sandpaper and apply paste wax.

Next, examine the set of the saw. If it is too slight, the blade can't pass through the kerf freely. An uneven set to the teeth will cause the cut to wander. Dullness, obviously,

Cut at an angle until you're just shy of the baseline.

FOLLOW BOTH LINES. Maintain the angle of the saw and sight down the scribe lines as you cut.

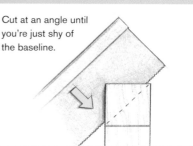

RIP THE CHEEKS. Use your fingernail to guide the saw and begin cutting at an acute angle to the workpiece.

The kerf guides the saw through the remainder of the cut.

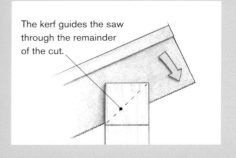

FINISH THE CUT. Flatten out your stroke to be parallel with the floor and saw to the shoulder cut.

is another reason. Teeth that are not jointed correctly, meaning the tips of the teeth are at different heights, will cause the saw to bounce and will not give a smooth cut. The obvious fix is to joint, reset the teeth, and sharpen.

Finally, look at your technique for sawing. If you crowd the cut with your body, as explained before, your saw will be more difficult to control.

With proper setup and technique, and a little practice, you will be able to control your saw and make accurate cuts.

PHILIP C. LOWE has been woodworking since 1968. In 1985 he opened a furniture shop in Beverly, Massachusetts, and has his own woodworking school, The Furniture Institute of Massachusetts.

Sources

Woodcraft
800-535-4482
Offers a sharpening service.

Accurate Joinery Starts with a Marking Knife

BY MARIO RODRIGUEZ

One of the secrets to achieving fine, crisp work is to lay out the joints carefully. Whether you're cutting with machines or by hand, working to a single clean line is essential. Instead of relying on a thick, blurry pencil line, I work to a reliable scribed line cut into the wood surface. Alongside smudged fingerprints, sweat stains, and wood dust, it remains unmistakable.

A marking knife cuts a straight, accurate line, highlighting exactly where to stop your cut. Besides offering a clear visual reference, this fine groove also leaves a positive starting point for any wood removal. On antique furniture the remnants of the craftsman's layout lines are often taken as visible proof that the piece was handmade.

Marking Knife Has Many Uses

A marking knife is so versatile that you need at least one in the shop. It can be used for hardware installation, for inlay work, for scoring cutlines to avoid blowout, and for laying out dovetails.

Marking Knife vs. Marking Gauge

Shortly after abandoning the pencil, many woodworkers take up the marking gauge. The traditional type of marking gauge scores a line into a board's surface with a stylus-like point that tends to tear wood fibers rather than cut them, often leaving a crude and ragged groove.

The marking gauge works best when used with the grain or on end grain, and when the desired line is close to a parallel edge. A good example is marking the cheeks of a tenon. However, the farther the cutter on a marking gauge is extended from its fence, the greater its tendency to wander. An example of this is marking out tenon shoulders. In this situation, the best tool is the marking knife. Used with a square, the marking knife easily cuts a clean, square shoulder line across the grain.

ON THE SHOULDERS THE MARKING GAUGE FALLS SHORT. It tears fibers when used cross-grain and far from its reference edge.

A MARKING GAUGE WORKS WELL FOR TENON CHEEKS. The cut is clean because it is with the grain and not far from the fence of the tool.

A KNIFE IS A BETTER TOOL FOR THE JOB. The marking knife leaves a flawless line, regardless of grain direction.

Using a Marking Knife

WELL-FIT DOVETAILS START WITH ACCURATE LAYOUT. A marking knife allows you to transfer the tail layout precisely onto the pins board. The thin incisions will guide the chisel later during final paring.

SCRIBE A LINE FOR CLEAN CUTS ON PLYWOOD. Cut this line into the bottom of the panel, where the sawteeth will exit.

MARKING OUT A HINGE MORTISE. The marking knife adds precision to this operation, too. The line will serve as a starting place for final chisel cuts around the perimeter.

When setting hinges, locks, and other hardware, not only does the marking knife produce a clear outline for the shallow mortise, but it also provides a fine notch for your chisel tip when you're removing the last of the waste.

A more advanced use of the marking knife is setting inlay and marquetry into a wood surface. Just as when mortising hinges, accurate work becomes as easy as putting the item in place, cutting a fine line around it and removing the waste.

A marking knife can also be used to eliminate blowout on the back of veneered panels or plywood being cut on the tablesaw or bandsaw. For clean crosscuts, cut a layout line across the bottom exactly at the panel's final dimension.

For me, however, the most indispensable use of the marking knife is laying out handcut dovetails. One of the keys to a gap-free fit is crisp, careful layout. Once I mark out the joint, the single line left by the marking knife provides the perfect boundary. The waste outside that line seems to flake away as I pare at it with a chisel, leaving only a clean dovetail recess or a precise pin.

There Are Several Types of Marking Knives

The most obvious distinction between marking knives is the way in which the blade is sharpened. The most common type used for marking has one side of the blade beveled, so the flat side of the blade can be placed vertically against a straightedge. Knives also can be sharpened on both sides of the blade. When using a double-beveled knife, you should angle the knife so that the bevel rests flat against the straightedge.

Another significant design difference is whether the blade has a single cutting edge or if the knife's tip is spear-shaped with two cutting edges. Generally, the two-edged knife has a sturdier tip and when rotated

180 degrees it can be used to scribe a line down the left or right side of an edge.

In the catalogs you'll find a wide variety of knives for marking. Some feature stout, mirror-polished blades attached to rosewood handles and are made to last a few lifetimes. Others are plastic-handled carving or specialty knives. In the shop, I've used everything from utility knives to X-Acto® blades. My favorite is a No. 1 chip-carving knife with a custom walnut handle shaped to fit my hand.

I use the fixed-blade, chip-carving blade for marking joinery and dovetails and a No. 1 X-Acto knife for marquetry and veneer work. Although I could get by with one knife, each type seems to be well suited to a particular type of work.

Sharpen on a Grinder or a Stone

I typically sharpen my fixed-blade knives on the bench grinder. Grinding the blade every time might shorten its life somewhat, but it saves me significant time over honing.

Of course, you can hone the blade using flat stones. This method might take a little longer, but it removes less material, leaves a finer edge, and eliminates the possibility of damaging the hardness by overheating the metal.

Whether it's single- or double-bevel, handled or handleless, ground or honed, a sharp marking knife will add accuracy to your work.

MARIO RODRIGUEZ is a contributing editor to *Fine Woodworking* magazine and the author of *Building Fireplace Mantels* (Taunton Press, 2002).

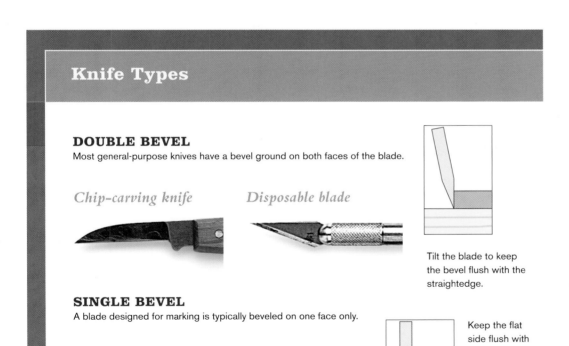

Knife Types

DOUBLE BEVEL
Most general-purpose knives have a bevel ground on both faces of the blade.

Chip-carving knife   *Disposable blade*

Tilt the blade to keep the bevel flush with the straightedge.

SINGLE BEVEL
A blade designed for marking is typically beveled on one face only.

Spear-point marking knife

Keep the flat side flush with the straightedge.

Hammers and Mallets

BY MARIO RODRIGUEZ

16-OZ. STRAIGHT-CLAW HAMMER
This hammer is great for heavy work in the shop: assembling large-scale dovetails, driving lag bolts before wrenching them, and setting the pronged drive center for a lathe into a blank. The head and handle are one piece, making this hammer a favorite among the pros because of its indestructible nature. At 21 years, this is my oldest hammer.

Fine woodworking is usually characterized by the careful cutting and fitting of joints that then slide together with only hand pressure. However, sometimes a little coercion is the most efficient response to a stubborn joint. In my shop I employ a variety of hammers and mallets to help me in a multitude of tasks: interior demolition and disassembly of existing work, dry-fitting of carcases, built-in installations and adjustment of tools such as the blades on molding planes. My favorite hammers and mallets are laid out here, along with explanations of what I use them for.

MARIO RODRIGUEZ is a contributing editor to *Fine Woodworking* magazine and the author of *Building Fireplace Mantels* (Taunton Press, 2002).

20-OZ. STRAIGHT-CLAW HAMMER
I use this heavy bruiser for construction and installation. The weight and length of this hammer are sufficient to drive an 8d common nail in two blows. The straight claw is useful for chipping stuff out of corners as well as for prying things apart. I prefer a fiberglass handle for a tight and permanent fit with the head; the rubber sheath gives a nonslip grip.

12-OZ. CURVED-CLAW HAMMER
For light assembly, this hammer's compact size reduces the chance of causing inadvertent damage. The red-oak handle feels good, but I have had to tighten it with oak shims a couple of times. The curved claw gives good leverage for pulling out nails without destroying the work.

JAPANESE HAMMER
This hammer is useful for setting the irons in Japanese planes, and for woodworking in tight corners. The head is of cast steel with a handle fitted through the eye and held tightly with wedges.

12-OZ. BALL-PEEN HAMMER
A small-scale, machine-shop staple comes in handy in my woodshop. There is always some bit of metal needing to be coaxed into place or straightened out. This hammer also does more mundane duty, such as tamping down paint-can lids.

6-OZ. TACK HAMMER
When I picked up this hammer almost 20 years ago at a five-and-dime store, I replaced the original, flimsy lauan handle with a hickory one. Now I love the feel of this tool. It is perfect for restoration work such as setting small, solid-wood patches and inlays. I also use it for setting wedges into joints and for adjusting blades and cutters on my antique planes.

CROSS-PEEN HAMMERS
Also known as a Warrington hammer, this style is considered a versatile shop hammer, as evidenced by the wide range of sizes it comes in. I use the 3½-oz. hammer (right) for delicate tasks such as nailing brads in picture frames, while the 12-oz. size (left) does universal duty. The tapered peen—the end of the head opposite the main striking head—can be used for starting small nails with less chance of hitting your fingers.

2-LB. MASON'S LUMP HAMMER
I use this brute for light demolition work such as removing interior trim and woodwork. It also provides just the right force for assembling the undercarriage of my Windsor chairs. I replaced the original handle with one made of hickory.

LAMINATED MALLET

The head on this mallet comprises $\frac{1}{16}$-in.-thick layers of laminated beech, making it stronger, heavier, and less prone to splitting than a solid-wood mallet. The face of this mallet is designed to strike the work at a more efficient angle than a square-headed mallet would.

DEADBLOW HAMMER

This rubber mallet features a hollow head filled with lead shot that delivers a solid blow without damaging the work. It doesn't have much visual or tactile appeal, but it's good for assembling large carcases.

LIGNUM VITAE CARVER'S MALLET

I use this when cutting mortises and carving. Unlike the square mallet, the round shape of this tool allows me to pick it up without having to orient its face to the work. I bought this mallet for $2 because of its crooked handle, but I wouldn't part with it for $20.

BRASS-HEADED MALLET

This mallet definitely punches above its weight. I use this compact tool mostly for carving because its ergonomic shape reduces fatigue. An added bonus of its small size is that it takes up less space in a tool bag.

A Basic Layout Kit

BY HORST J. MEISTER

I was 15 years old when I built my first cabinet. Shortly before my mother's birthday, I overheard her tell my father that she would really like to have a little cabinet for her sewing room. The very next Saturday, I locked myself in the garage with a generous supply of redwood boards, a bent aluminum yardstick, a box of dowels, glue, a crosscut saw, and three Snickers candy bars.

The finished piece fell a little shy of my expectations. Believing that square corners were a very desirable feature in furniture, my dad gave me a try square for my 16th birthday. Soon, my woodworking projects improved to the point that people other than my mother liked what I made.

A good try square, a ruler, and a marking knife are the fundamental layout tools that few serious woodworkers can get along without. Add a marking gauge or mortising gauge, a bevel gauge, a protractor, and a set of dividers and trammels and you'll have a basic layout kit. Why spend the money? Good-quality layout tools will last a lifetime, and flawed measurements will plague a project through every stage. Even small errors are a detraction if they occur in a prominent place.

I have obtained excellent results in woodwork using some of the machinist's layout tools that are standard equipment in the tool-and-die industry. And they often cost less than comparable tools specifically designed for woodworkers. They're not as pretty as the best woodworker's tools. However, good looks don't get the job done—accuracy does.

Start with a Try Square or an Engineer's Square

The try square is a very simple device. It's just a thin metal blade permanently set at 90 degrees to a thicker wood or metal handle. Its uses are many: You can check the

squareness of milled stock, mark square shoulders, lay out joinery, or check the accuracy of the miter gauge on your table-saw or the fence on your jointer. Without a good try square, you can't make anything square. A number of companies make try squares specifically for woodworkers. They vary in price and appearance, but you don't need to spend a lot of money.

COMBINATION SQUARES JUST DON'T MEASURE UP. **The handle is shorter than that on a try square, giving less support when marking a line.**

ENGINEER'S SQUARES ARE STURDY AND ACCURATE. They're useful for checking machine fences and blades because their wide handles make them stable on edge.

USE A BEVEL GAUGE FOR LAYOUT TASKS BEYOND 90 DEGREES. **With few variations, the design has remained the same for a hundred years. The Starrett No. 47 on the left has been in production since 1891.**

For super accuracy and durability, consider using an engineer's square with a 12-in. blade (see the bottom left photo on the facing page). The handle and blade are hardened and then silver-soldered together. These squares can't get out of alignment unless you subject them to serious abuse, like pounding on them with a large hammer. In the 12-in. size, most brands are guaranteed to be square to 0.0025 in. (1/400 in.) or less. Chinese engineer's squares are not as good as U.S., English, German, or Japanese squares.

Combination squares (see the top photo on the facing page) have their uses. Because the blade is adjustable, it can fit into a tight place or reach that extra inch a try square can't. Despite these advantages, they're not entirely suitable for use as a try square for two reasons. First, the bearing surface of a standard 90-degree combination-square head is shorter than that of an engineer's or try square's handle, which is typically 80% as long as the blade. The extra length gives better leverage against cutting pressure on the blade while marking. The relative shortness of the combination square's head makes it easier for you to push the blade off the desired line. Second, the blade and head on a combination square will wear against each other over time and eventually go out of square.

Next, an Accurate Metal Ruler

A good ruler should have fine, crisp graduations that are cut into the metal and contrast with their background. Aluminum rulers with usable graduations are available for a reasonable price at most hardware stores. However, aluminum is a soft metal that is easily scratched or bent. When used for scribing lines, sharp marking knives will nick the edge of an aluminum ruler.

WHERE EXACTLY IS 1⅜ IN.? Time and use have taken their toll on this steel tape measure (top) and this folding rule (bottom). Not designed to last, the graduations have worn from the edges of both. The tape measure's hook bends easily, and the rivets wear loose. Use a precision ruler when accuracy counts.

CHOOSE A RULER FOR ITS LONGEVITY AND ACCURACY. The painted graduations on the soft aluminum ruler (top) will not fare well with use, but the etched graduations on the steel ruler (bottom) are more precise and will last a long time.

For a few dollars more, you can buy a machinist's ruler, which is a far superior tool (see the bottom photo). Available in lengths from 6 in. to 48 in., these scales are made of hardened stainless steel and have very accurate graduations. Starrett, Brown & Sharpe®, Rabone Chesterman, and Mitutoyo® rulers have finely cut graduations accurate to within a few thousandths per foot. A set, consisting of a 6-in., an 18-in., and a 36-in. ruler with fractional graduations, will handle most measurement tasks.

Steel measuring tapes are convenient, reasonably priced, and handy. However, they're not accurate enough for cabinet work. The rivets that fasten the sliding hook to the end of the tape wear with use, making the tape less and less accurate (see the top photo on p. 55). Most measuring tapes have painted graduations that may wear off. Folding rules have many of the same drawbacks, most notably painted graduations and joints that can bind on sawdust or small shavings. Precision rulers have few of these limitations, but they can't measure long distances.

For Marking, Use a Knife, Not a Pencil

Pencil lines are too wide for accurate layout work, and the graphite tends to smear. Scoring the wood with a knife makes a precise mark that won't smudge or wear out. There are a number of different marking-knife designs on the market. I don't see much reason to choose one design over another as long as the knife leaves a clean, accurate cut and it's comfortable to use. The blade should be thin and very sharp at its tip so it can be held tightly against the blade of a square. Then the line can be knifed right along the edge.

AN AWL POINT breaks wood fibers across the grain; a sharp knife cuts them.

USE A PROTRACTOR TO SCRIBE ANY ANGLE but a right angle. Without superfine etched graduations on the head, finding an angle will be hit or miss. Cheap protractors can misguide you by several degrees.

Strive to make your layout marks in exactly the same manner each time. Hold the marking knife at the same angle relative to the ruler and the wood each time you mark the work. A knifed line should be deep enough to see easily. Yet it should be as light as possible to keep the knife blade from following the grain rather than the ruler.

Many furniture makers leave dovetail layout lines on drawer sides or cabinet faces as a sign the piece was made by hand. But ordinarily, you wouldn't use a marking knife on surfaces that will be exposed after assembly. Your best bet is the traditional carpenter's pencil with the lead sharpened to a knife-edged chisel point. The pencil's chisel point draws a cleaner line than the conical point on a standard pencil. And the pencil's rectangular body won't roll off your bench.

Some woodworkers prefer using an awl rather than a marking knife. Even when it's sharpened to a fine needle point, though, an awl suffers from a tendency to follow the wood's grain and crush fibers, not cut them (see the inset photo on the facing page). Marks scratched with an awl tend to be fuzzy, especially in softwoods.

Marking and Mortising Gauges

There are different kinds of marking gauges, but they all work on the same principle. The basic marking gauge consists of a steel cutter mounted on a beam that fits in a fence. A setscrew or wedge fixes the beam to the fence at whatever distance is desired. Marking gauges can have pins, small blades, even discs for cutters. Gauges that have blades are called cutting gauges.

Marking gauges are used to scribe a line parallel to an edge. Set the pin or knife to the distance to be marked and then tighten the fence to the beam with the setscrew or wedge. Hold the fence against the edge of the material with the pin touching the wood. Because the tool is guided by the edge of the work, any line that's cut with a

GOOD LIGHTING, A MAGNIFYING GLASS, AND CAREFUL FILING will greatly improve the performance of a pin gauge. The pin may be filed to a small knife edge, which won't tear the wood as much.

THE LARGER BLADE OF A CUTTING GAUGE will produce a cleaner cut across the grain.

marking gauge is certain to be parallel to that edge as long as the fence is held firmly against the work while the line is being cut.

The pin of a factory-sharpened gauge makes a fuzzy, irregular mark. Filing the tip to an oval-shaped knife edge makes it cut better. A pin filed to a slight angle helps draw the fence against the workpiece. For cutting across the grain, a cutting gauge does an even better job than a marking gauge. Even when the pin of a marking gauge is sharpened as described above, it can hop or tear out when marking across the grain. The alternating rings of soft sum-

mer and hard winter wood cause the gauge to do this. A cutting gauge's knife doesn't have this problem, but it needs a light touch to keep it from making a deeper cut than you need.

I prefer a marking gauge with a small disc for a cutter. Fastened to the end of the beam, the disc is about the size of a dime and has a bevel on the side facing the fence. A disc cutter combines the advantages of both pin and knife. It will mark equally well across and with the grain. The bevel pulls the fence against the stock as you draw the tool along the work, and the line it cuts is clean, straight, and sharply defined without being too deep.

A mortise gauge is simply a marking gauge with two independently adjustable cutters. It's used to make two parallel lay-out lines. To use one, first set the distance between the pins to the width of the mor-tise, and then set the beam to the mortise location on the workpiece. The two cutters outline the width of the mortise with one stroke of the gauge.

A Bevel Gauge or Protractor for Angles

A protractor is used to measure and deter-mine angles. It has a radial scale calibrated in degrees and an arm that pivots on the center point of the scale's radius. A protrac-tor can be set to any specified angle in its range, and the protractor's arm is then used to draw the set angle onto the stock. A good machinist's combination square set comes with a very accurate protractor that has a vernier caliper that allows you to measure angles as small as $\frac{1}{4}$ degree.

A protractor is useful for determining exact angles, but a bevel gauge is the pre-ferred tool for checking, comparing and transferring angles (see the bottom right photo on p. 54). Bevel gauges are similar to protractors in principle, having a handle and a sliding blade that can be adjusted to any angle, but they don't have a scale.

THE AUTHOR DRAWS HIS SHOPMADE DISC GAUGE TOWARD HIM. **The cutter (inset) does not spin freely, but when it dulls, it is easily turned to a fresh edge.**

Dividers and Trammels
for Circles and Arcs

Woodworking dividers are used for scribing
small circles and arcs (see the photo above).
The best dividers have a joint tensioned
with a bow spring and a fine-pitch adjusting screw. For best results, sharpen one of
the divider points to a sharp needle; this is
the point you will use as the axis to pivot
from. Sharpen the other point to an oval
knife shape, as on the marking gauge, with
the flat side of the knife shape at right angles to the main axis of the dividers. Sharpened in this fashion, dividers will cut an arc

as cleanly as a marking knife (see the photo
above).

A trammel is nothing more than two
sharp steel points (or a steel point and a
pencil point) mounted in heads that slide
on and clamp to a long beam. Trammel
heads equipped with an eccentric point
allow you to finely adjust the radius after
they have been clamped to the beam. The
trammel's great advantage over a divider is
that the radius of the circles it can draw is
limited only by the length of the beam. To
draw an arc with a 10 ft. radius, simply
mount the trammel heads on a beam that is
that long.

Besides drawing arcs and circles, both
dividers and trammels can be used to lay
out complex geometric shapes with a high
degree of accuracy. If you need to lay out a
hexagon, for example, you can do it with
dividers. Just draw a circle with the desired
radius, and without changing the setting of
the points, step the dividers around the cir-
cumference to divide it into six equal parts.
Then connect the intersection marks with
straight lines. You now have a pretty good
hexagon.

HORST J. MEISTER is a toolmaker and woodworker
who lives in Riverside, California.

The Combination Square: A Perfect Name for a Near Perfect Tool

BY ANTHONY GUIDICE

YOU GET WHAT YOU PAY FOR. A high-quality combination square costs about $70, but it's the most versatile woodworking tool you'll own. A high-quality square has exact machined edges, graduations that are machined, rather than stamped, into the sliding blade, and a solid-locking thumbscrew.

The combination square is the most versatile measuring tool there is. It is so valuable that I have my beginning students use it to the exclusion of all other measuring tools—at first. The tool teaches beginners the concept of accuracy in layouts and measurements. You mark a line and look at it. It isn't automatically square. Does it look square and straight? If it's not, you're the cause, not the tool. For a beginner, using a simple tool helps develop this concept. It keeps the mind uncluttered. Later, a student can use marking gauges, cutting gauges, and center markers. But far from just a great learning tool for woodworking students, the combination square is an indispensable little device for all woodworkers.

Use It as a Depth Gauge

A combination square works very well as a depth gauge and a thickness gauge. I use mine as a thickness gauge when I'm using a power plane. I lay a board flat on the workbench, loosen the thumbscrew on the square, and measure the distance between the top of the board and the bench. To measure the depth of a mortise, rest the square on the edge, extend the blade into the mortise and read the depth. To use it as a height indicator for a tablesaw blade, preset the depth you want and raise the tablesaw blade until a tooth at the top center contacts the square.

As a Marking Gauge

The combination square is a good substitute for a marking or cutting gauge. For hand ripping and planing, clamp the work in the bench first. Set the dimension on the square and lock it. Slide the square along

CHECK THE THICKNESS OF A BOARD. Loosen the thumbscrew of the square and measure from the top of the workbench to the top of the board.

USE A COMBINATION SQUARE AS A DEPTH GAUGE. To check the depth of a mortise, rest the head of the square on the face of your wood and lower the blade into the mortise.

THE SQUARE WORKS AS A MARKING GAUGE. Set the blade to the desired width, hold the head against the edge of a board, and, while holding a pencil at the end of the blade, slide the square along the edge of the board.

the edge of the board while guiding a marking knife or pencil with the edge of the blade. This takes practice, but you can get the hang of it pretty quickly. For mortises and tenons, mark with a sharp pencil on the work, adjust the square to that, and mark the whole joint with the knife. The same technique can be used to mark depth on the end of the board for hand-cutting dovetails.

CALIBRATE YOUR TABLESAW. Lock the blade at the 90° end of the head and hold the square against the edge of the sawblade, making sure the square's blade rests along the edge of the sawblade, not against one of the teeth.

As a Try Square and to Calibrate Your Tablesaw

An accurate combination square can also be used as a try square. It can measure inside corners or outside corners. Quite often I use my combination square for marking 90-degree crosscuts or 45-degree miters when I'm making a cut with a handsaw.

I calibrate my tablesaw with the combination square. Raise the blade all the way, then lock the combination-square blade flush with the corner and sight for 90 degrees by holding the square tight to the sawblade, making sure the square's blade isn't resting on the edge of any of the blade's teeth. Use the square without the blade to calibrate the 45-degree setting.

You can also use a combination square to check the squareness of your tablesaw blade to the miter-gauge slot. First, unplug your saw and raise the blade to its full height. Mark one of the saw teeth with chalk. Rotate the marked tooth to the front of the blade insert, rest one edge of the square in the miter slot, and extend the combination-square blade out to the tooth. Rotate the marked tooth to the back of the sawblade insert and check it with the square. If the blade tooth doesn't meet the square exactly as it did in front, you need to adjust the saw.

CHECK THE SQUARENESS OF THE SAW TABLE TO THE SAWBLADE. Hold the square tight to the miter slot and set the blade so that it just touches the edge of a blade tooth at the front of the blade insert. Rotate the blade, slide the square back and check the same tooth at the back of the insert. If the tooth doesn't meet the square exactly as it did in the front, your saw needs adjusting.

Or Set Your Router

I have a jig for cutting mortises with a plunge router, and I use a combination square to set the edge guide. I lock in the distance from the edge of the jig to the mortise on the combination square. I use that setting to set the distance from the bit to the edge guide. To rout dadoes, you can set the distance from the edge of the router base to the bit, then use that to set a straightedge clamp. In a router table you can use the combination square just as you did with the tablesaw blade to measure the depth of a cut.

Quality Costs and Quality Counts

An important consideration when buying a combination square is its quality. Good ones can cost upward of $70, but they are worth their weight in gold. Poor-quality combination squares are fine for rough carpentry like framing, but you really need a high-quality square for precise work. Errors accumulate very quickly in woodworking, particularly in machine work. If you start measuring inaccurately and making cuts, before you know it one side of your work could end up being ³⁄₁₆ in. shorter than the other.

There are several things to look for when acquiring a combination square. The sliding blade of a good square is heavy and stiff, and the measurement graduations are machined into the blade rather than stamped. The square's head—the part that holds the blade—should have an easy-to-use locking thumbscrew that holds the blade with viselike rigidity.

There is also a difference in how a high-quality combination square works. An accurate combination square is absolute in its indications; you can very easily tell if the work is on the mark or not. By comparison, measurements from a poor-quality combination square aren't clearly defined

USE IT AS A ROUTER GAUGE. It's easy to check the base-to-bit distance on your router. You can then use the square to set up a straightedge for routing dadoes.

because either the measurement graduations aren't easily read or the measurements aren't accurate.

As I've said, a good-quality combination square is versatile: Use it as a depth gauge, a marking gauge, a square, and a ruler. The sliding blade can also be removed from the head and used as a short straightedge or as a handy ruler. A final note, and this is important: Never, never, never use the blade of your combination square as a mini prybar or to pop open a paint can. Although if you want to stretch the meaning of "combination" and possibly ruin the trueness of the blade, it will work quite well for those tasks, too.

ANTHONY GUIDICE builds custom furniture and teaches woodworking in St. Louis, Missouri.

Shopmade Squares

BY GARY WILLIAMS

A good square is an indispensable tool in the shop. So it makes sense to have several of them within easy reach of your workbench. For checking small parts, a 2-in. machinist's square is a good choice. As parts get bigger, a 6-in. try square or 12-in. combination square is nice to have. And for larger parts, a framing square comes in handy.

But there can be a need for a shop square that's size somewhere between a combination square and a framing square. For an especially big project, like a cupboard, it would be handy to have a shop square that's even bigger than a framing square.

Unfortunately, you can't run to the hardware store to get such odd-size shop squares. And you won't find them in a mail-order catalog or at any nearby woodworking store. So I decided to make my own. That way I could size the shop squares to suit my needs to a tee.

Just One Word: Plastics

To be of any real value, a shop square needs to be dead accurate. So when making one, it's best to use a stable material that won't warp when the relative humidity starts changing. I ended up choosing acrylic plastic sheet, a product sold under trade names such as Plexiglas® and Lucite®.

Don't worry if you haven't cut acrylic sheet before. A sharp, 60-tooth, carbide-tipped combination blade does a nice job. The acrylic colors you're most likely to find locally are white or clear, but more interesting colors are available from suppliers like Ridout Plastics. Ridout will ship you a 2-ft. by 4-ft. piece, which provides more than enough material to make the four squares shown on the facing page. You can also order the acrylic sheet online at www.ridoutplastics.com.

You'll also need to order special glue for acrylic plastic. The easiest to use is a water-thin product called Weld-On® No. 3. It's used with a squeeze bottle that has a needle applicator and is drawn into the joint after clamping.

One Design, Four Squares

Each of these shop squares uses a three-piece laminated handle, with the blade inserted and glued into the middle of the laminations. This construction provides a nice, thick handle like that on a try square, which I find much easier to use than a one-piece framing square. It also ensures a strong connection between the two legs of the tool.

The procedure for building these shop squares can be broken down into four basic steps. First build a glue-up jig. Next, make a plywood testing square and use it to square the jig. Third, cut out the blade and handle parts and glue up the handles. Finally, use the glue-up jig to assemble each blade and handle so that they end up perfectly square.

Square Construction

The squares are made from ¼-in.-thick acrylic plastic, a material that resists warping. Acrylic sheets can be cut on the tablesaw using a 60-tooth, carbide-tipped combination blade.

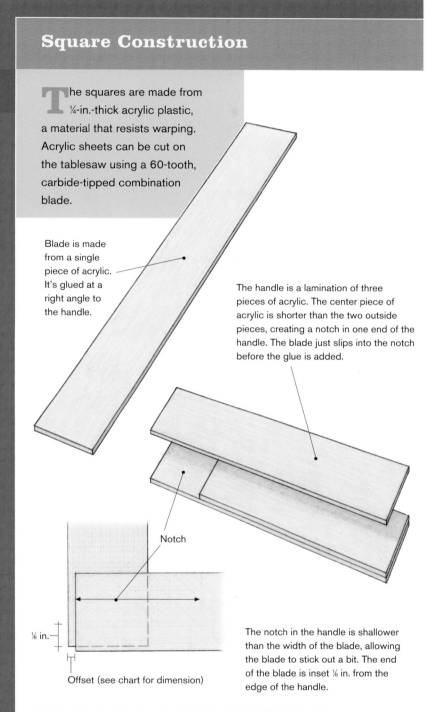

Blade is made from a single piece of acrylic. It's glued at a right angle to the handle.

The handle is a lamination of three pieces of acrylic. The center piece of acrylic is shorter than the two outside pieces, creating a notch in one end of the handle. The blade just slips into the notch before the glue is added.

Notch

⅛ in.

Offset (see chart for dimension)

The notch in the handle is shallower than the width of the blade, allowing the blade to stick out a bit. The end of the blade is inset ⅛ in. from the edge of the handle.

SQUARE DIMENSIONS

SIZE	BLADE	HANDLE	OFFSET
48 in.	3½ in. by 48 in.	3½ in. by 24 in.	½ in.
30 in.	3 in. by 30 in.	3 in. by 17½ in.	⅜ in.
20 in.	2½ in. by 20 in.	2½ in. by 11½ in.	¼ in.
12 in.	2 in. by 12 in.	2 in. by 6½ in.	¼ in.

A Glue-Up Jig Ensures a Perfect 90 Degree Angle

The blade and handle of the square are assembled on a simple, two-piece jig made up of a reference board that's mounted exactly 90 degrees to the lower edge of the base. To get the jig angle just right, you need the aid of a testing square.

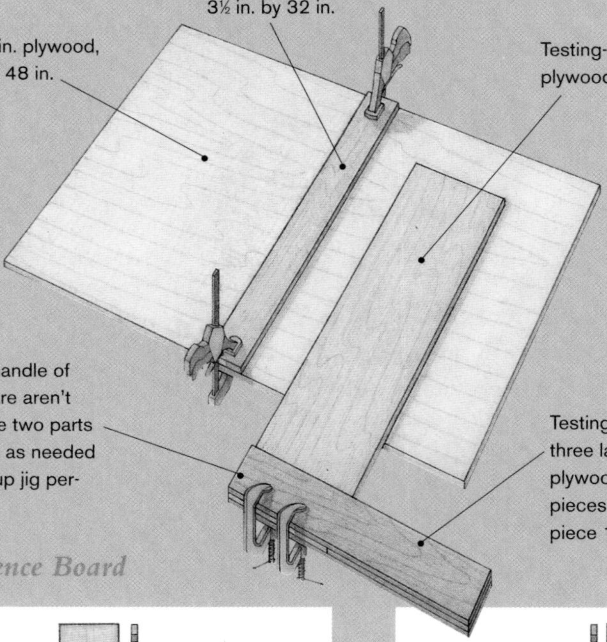

Reference board, ½-in. plywood, 3½ in. by 32 in.

Base, ¾-in. plywood, 32 in. by 48 in.

Testing-square blade, ½-in. plywood, 8 in. by 40 in.

The blade and handle of the testing square aren't glued so that the two parts can be adjusted as needed to get the glue-up jig perfectly square.

Testing-square handle, three layers of ½-in. plywood, 3¾ in. wide (two pieces 21 in. long; one piece 17½ in. long)

Use the Testing Square to Align the Reference Board

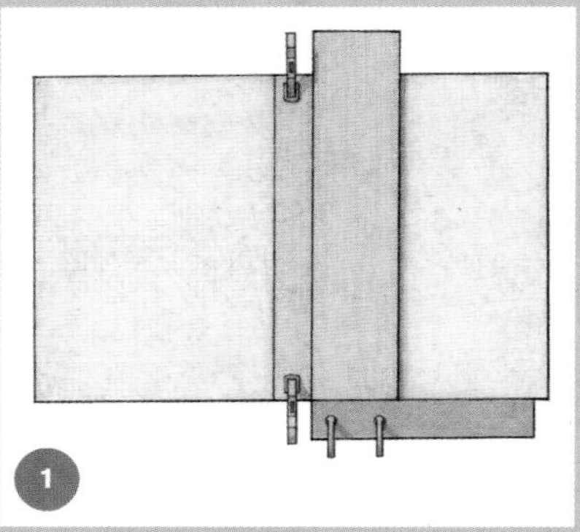

1 **CLAMP THE REFERENCE BOARD ROUGHLY SQUARE TO THE BOTTOM EDGE OF THE BASE.** Loosen one of the two clamps on the testing square while holding the handle against the bottom edge of the base. Then pivot the blade until it butts to the reference board.

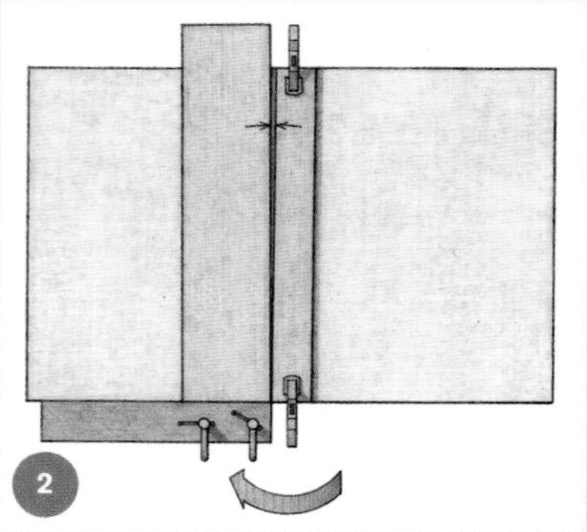

2 **FLIP THE TESTING SQUARE. The gap that shows is exactly twice the amount that the parts are out of square. Pivot the reference board to remove about one-half the gap. Then adjust the testing square flush with the reference board.**

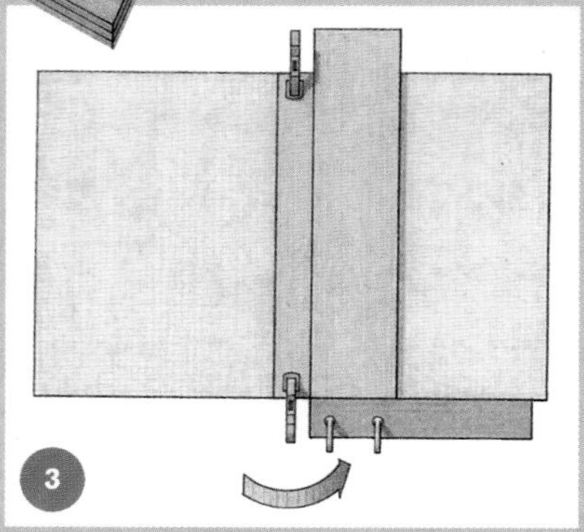

3 **FLOP THE TESTING SQUARE TO THE OTHER SIDE OF THE REFERENCE BOARD AND REPEAT THE ADJUSTMENT STEPS.** Continue the flip-flop steps as needed, until the gap is completely gone. Three or four adjustments usually get the job done.

Make a glue-up jig This is really just two pieces of plywood, but it is the heart of this project. A true reference board laid exactly perpendicular to a true edge becomes an "index" for calibrating all your new squares. When the blade of a square is glued to the handle, the jig squares the two parts and keeps them that way until the glue dries.

For the jig to be accurate, the bottom edge of the base must be perfectly straight. Use the factory edge of good-quality plywood or medium-density fiberboard

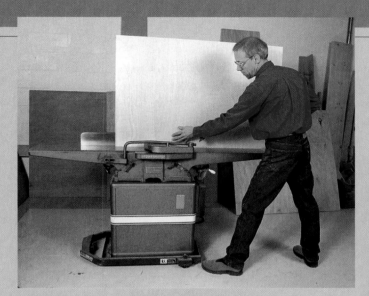

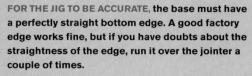

FOR THE JIG TO BE ACCURATE, the base must have a perfectly straight bottom edge. A good factory edge works fine, but if you have doubts about the straightness of the edge, run it over the jointer a couple of times.

CHECK THE REFERENCE BOARD FOR PARALLEL. The width of the reference board should be the same within a few thousandths of an inch along the board's length. If you have a caliper, this is a good time to use it.

A TESTING SQUARE IS USED TO SQUARE UP THE JIG. A long blade and notched handle make up the testing square. When the two parts are clamped together, the glue-up jig is ready to be squared.

(MDF). If you have a large jointer, you can run the edge over it just to be sure.

It is also important for both of the long edges of the reference board to be straight and parallel. Once the reference board has been ripped, measure its width carefully at several places along the length. Use a caliper if you have one.

To complete the jig, the reference board has to be clamped square to the base. To do that precisely you need to make one more helper—a testing square.

Make a testing square Like the shop squares, the testing square has a blade and a laminated handle. But instead of acrylic plastic, the testing square is made of ½-in. plywood. And it differs from the plastic versions in one other important way—the blade isn't permanently attached to the handle. Instead, it simply slips into the notch in the handle and is held in place by a pair of clamps. The clamps can be loosened, allowing the blade to pivot in the handle, and that's the secret to using the testing square to square the glue-up jig. I'll talk more about this later.

Rip a 4-ft.-long blade and three pieces to make the handle. Size is not critical, but make this square big enough to be sturdy. Then glue up the three-part handle. And as has been the general rule from the get-go here, straight and parallel is the goal. So when the glue dries, rip both sides of the assembly again.

Squaring the glue-up jig now becomes a matter of flip-flopping. First position the reference board so that it's roughly perpendicular to the bottom edge of the base. Hold it temporarily in place with a clamp on each end.

Now you're ready to calibrate. Position the testing square on the jig and pivot its blade to snug up against the reference board. Clamp the square in this position.

Flop the square over to the other side of the reference board. Unless you have remarkable luck, you're going to see a gap between the board and the square, either close to the handle or out at the end of the blade.

To begin correcting this out-of-squareness, loosen one clamp on the reference board and pivot it to remove approximately half the gap. Retighten the clamp. Then loosen the clamps on the testing square and again pivot the blade to exactly match the angle of the reference board.

Now flop the testing square back to the other side of the reference board and repeat the procedure, removing half the error each time. It might take a few of these flip-flop adjustments, but you'll soon find, on both sides of the reference board, that the edge of the blade butts along the entire length of the board. When that happens, the reference board is exactly square to the bottom edge of the base. And the jig is ready to use.

Cut and glue up the plastic parts With the glue-up jig completed, you're ready to start making the four shop squares. The first thing to do is rip and crosscut the parts for all four squares. Rip the parts a little wide, say about ³⁄₁₆ in., so that they can be ripped true after lamination. By the way, if you start with a 2-ft. by 4-ft. piece, you're going to have enough material left over to cut one or two more squares.

Before you begin cutting, raise the blade fairly high above the saw table. That gets the cutting edge of the blade closer to 90 degrees, which helps produce a better cut in acrylics. And to avoid overheating the plastic, push it as quickly as possible through the blade. As always, use eye protection—those bits of cut plastic are hard, and they like to fly. And keep your fingers well away from that raised blade.

Once the parts have been cut out, glue up the three pieces that make up each of the handles. But before starting, it's helpful here to understand how the Weld-On No. 3 glue is applied. Just run the end of the needle applicator along the joint line, squeezing a narrow bead of glue as you go. The glue immediately gets drawn deep into the joint to form a strong bond.

To make it easier to follow the joint line with the needle applicator, you'll want to add a little chamfer to the mating edges of the handle parts. That way, when the handle parts are fitted together, the chamfers create a little groove that positions the needle directly over the joint.

Make the Handle

CUT THE HANDLE PARTS. A sharp, 60-tooth, carbide-tipped combination blade cuts the acrylic sheet without much fuss. The paper backing on the sheet helps reduce chipout, plus it protects the plastic from getting scratched.

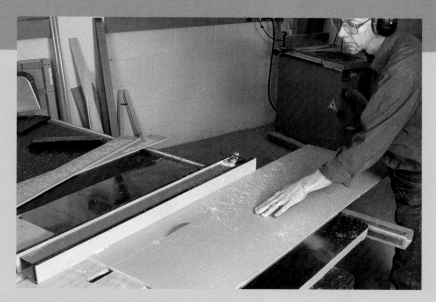

CHAMFER THE EDGES. The water-thin glue, used to join the three parts of each handle comes in a squeeze bottle with a needle applicator. Sanding a light chamfer along the mating edges of the handle parts creates a shallow groove when the parts are joined together.

ASSEMBLE AND GLUE THE HANDLE. Secure the handle parts with spring clamps and check to make sure that all of the edges remain flush. With the sanded groove as a guide, run a bead of glue all along the joint lines on the handle. The glue is pulled deep into the joint and quickly forms a sturdy bond.

Assemble the Square Using the Glue-Up Jig

AFTER CUTTING THE BLADE TO SIZE, IT'S TIME TO PUT THE JIG TO USE. But first, to help support the handle during the glue-up, clamp a scrap piece to the corner of the jig. (1) Assemble the blade to the handle, then hold the handle to the bottom edge of the jig and butt the blade against the reference board. (2) A stick of scrap stock clamped to the base of the jig keeps the blade from shifting during the glue-up. (3) When the blade and handle are properly positioned, a pair of clamps is added. (4) Use the needle applicator to apply the glue to the joint lines connecting the handle and blade.

Hold the three parts together with some clamps. Then it's just a matter of running the bead of glue along all of the joint lines.

After all of the handles have been glued up, rip both edges again and crosscut a bit off the ends, so that the finished assembly is straight and parallel.

At this point, the hard work is done. All that's left to do is attach the blades to the handles, a step that's just about foolproof, thanks to the glue-up jig.

To help support the end of the handle, it's a good idea to clamp a piece of scrap stock to the corner of the jig. Then add a smaller scrap to serve as a spacer, which helps level the handle.

To join the parts, just slip a blade into a mating handle. Position the end of the blade so that it ends up about ⅛ in. short of the outside edge of the handle. That way the end of the blade won't stick out and get in the way when using your shop square to check an inside corner.

Now, with the handle firmly against the base of the glue-up jig, pivot the blade so that its edge is pressed against the reference board. Clamp the joint to hold the two parts in position and apply a bead of glue all along the joint lines.

Keep the parts in the jig until the glue starts to set up. A couple of minutes should be enough time. After that, set the clamped square in a safe place and allow it to dry overnight.

With the assembly completed, only a few things remain to be done. To soften the sharp edges of your new shop squares, round over the edges ever so slightly with some 220-grit sandpaper. Then, drill a hole in the handle and find a good spot on your shop wall to hang them.

GARY WILLIAMS is a technical writer, woodworker, and new grandpa living in San Diego, California.

Shopmade Marking Gauge

BY JOHN NESSET

When I set out as a woodworker, a marking gauge was one of the first tools I bought. A straight line parallel to a straight edge is—along with a perfect right angle—the foundation of woodworking. No matter how you eventually shape a piece, if your layout lines aren't true, that table will not stand level, that drawer will not open smoothly, and those joints will be sloppy. After examining several marking gauges, I chose one made of rosewood with brass hardware, inlaid brass wear plates, and graceful scrolling on its faces. It was a handsome tool that came in a nice box. However, I found it difficult to use.

For one thing, making adjustments required tightening and loosening a thumb-screw, an awkward procedure when I also had to hold the fence in place. In use, it was difficult to keep the short fence running snug against the edge of the board. Hard or soft spots in the wood and diverging grain patterns grabbed the pin and made it skip or go off track. I usually had to go over lines several times, with miscues marring the stock.

About that time, back in the mid-1970s, Japanese tools began to appear in the popular woodworking catalogs. I marveled at their simple but clever designs, but I didn't find many of them adaptable to my Western woodworking techniques. There were, however, two notable exceptions. The first was those wonderful, precise pull saws, and the other was the *kebiki*, a Japanese marking gauge. My first pass with it was a spiritual moment.

The Tool Has Four Parts

The size and shape of the arm/wedge mortise and the knife slot are critical, but the other contours are up to you.

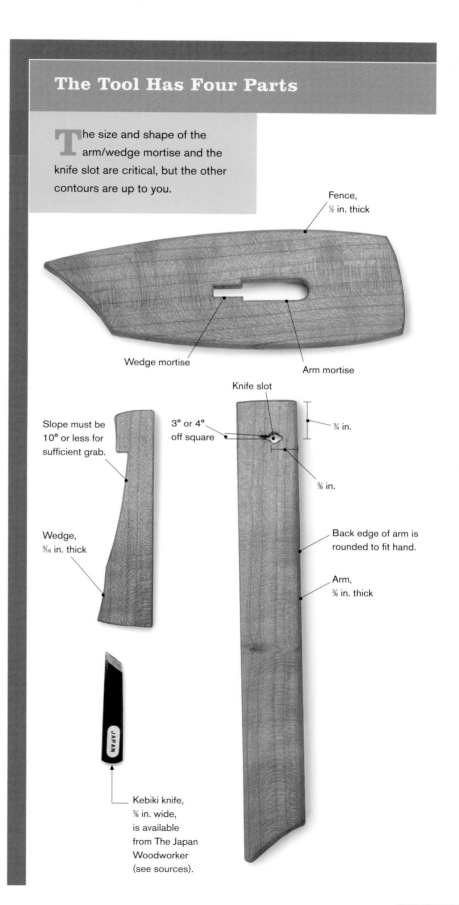

Fence, ⅛ in. thick

Wedge mortise

Arm mortise

Slope must be 10° or less for sufficient grab.

Wedge, ³⁄₁₆ in. thick

Knife slot

3° or 4° off square

¾ in.

⅜ in.

Back edge of arm is rounded to fit hand.

Arm, ⅜ in. thick

Kebiki knife, ⅜ in. wide, is available from The Japan Woodworker (see sources).

Adjust the Marking Gauge

FINE ADJUSTMENTS ARE MADE WITH ONE HAND. Light taps on the benchtop adjust the arm, and another quick tap tightens the wedge. It takes a little experimentation to get used to the interplay between the two parts.

Easy Adjustment and No Skipping

The kebiki is a perfect piece of engineering. A wedge holds the fence in place on the arm. Precise adjustments are made by tapping one end of the arm or the other on the workbench while holding the kebiki in one hand and checking against a measuring device or workpiece held in your other hand. And the marking process is trouble-free, thanks to the long fence and the design of the pin.

The pin is actually a small knife that is beveled on one side—away from the fence—and set in the arm at a slight angle. The result of this design is that the blade wants to pull away from the fence, drawing the gauge snugly against the workpiece. Irregularities in the wood will not divert the sharp blade, and it leaves a clean mark.

My kebiki became a true friend I could always count on. I find it indispensable for a number of common tasks, such as marking the depth of cut for dovetails, marking dadoes and rabbets, marking mortises or tenons from a straight edge, marking grooves on the inner edges of frames for accepting panels, and marking the thickness or width of stock once one side has been planed flat and straight.

Making a Kebiki

The kebiki I purchased so many years ago was made of Japanese white oak, but any hardwood will do. The fence should be about ½ in. thick, the arm around ⅜ in. thick, and the wedge about 3/16 in. thick (see the sidebar on p. 73). If you are left-handed, reverse the orientation of the arm and knife.

Cut the Arm Mortise

START WITH PAPER PATTERNS. Use them to find the best grain location for each part. Then use the fence pattern to lay out the mortise for the arm.

USE A MARKING GAUGE TO LAY OUT THE SIDES. A ⅜-in.-dia. hole defines the rounded end. The mortise extends from the edges of the hole.

CHOP OUT THE REST. Insert one corner of the arm stock to test the width of the mortise.

Two important mortises After thicknessing the stock, use paper templates to find pleasing grain areas for each part and trace their outlines. Before cutting the fence to its final curved shape, lay out and cut the mortises for the arm and the wedge. The arm will be rounded on its back edge to sit comfortably in the hand during use. That means the mortise for the arm must also be rounded at one end. Start by drilling a ⅜-in.-dia. hole through the fence and then marking the rest of the mortise off that. Chop out the mortise, checking it against the thickness of the arm stock.

The wedge securing the arm to the fence is a critical element. The angle should not exceed 10 degrees, and the mortise that it wedges against should be cut to exactly the same angle. Cut the wedge first, then use it to determine the angle of the mortise wall.

WHEN THE ARM AND WEDGE MORTISES ARE COMPLETE, cut out the arm and fence. The author shapes the roughsawn parts with hand tools, using a shallow gouge and a block plane.

Cut the Wedge Mortise

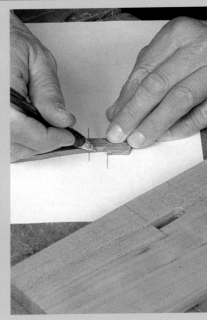

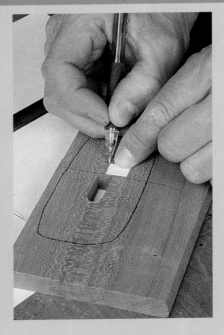

MORE FUN WITH PAPER. To make an accurate angled mortise, start by tracing the thickness of the fence onto paper.

THEN OVERLAY THE WEDGE to trace a cross section of the mortise needed. Use the narrowest portion of the wedge.

THE RESULTING PAPER BLOCK now contains the exact lengths of each side of the angled mortise. Lay out each side and chop out the mortise.

After giving the edges of the mortises a slight bevel to protect them, you can shape the fence block. I saw out the rough outline and then smooth it with a block plane or spokeshave rather than with sandpaper. The tool marks give the kebiki character, and they remain there as a satisfying reminder of the work you did.

Finally, saw and shape the ends of the arm, and use a block plane to round its back edge. Before rounding this edge to fit its ⅜-in. mortise, lay out lines ¾₆ in. down from the edge on each side, to guide your work. When you reach these lines, the rounded profile should be correct. A little fine-tuning of the arm and wedge gets them working smoothly in the fence block.

Adding the knife Kebiki knives, made of laminated steel, are now available for under $10★, but I've also had success adapting a Japanese marking knife. In fact, any piece of good steel will work. Grind the edge to a shallow angle (without overheating the steel) and hacksaw it off at the desired length. Always leave enough length to grip when resharpening the blade. (I use locking pliers to remove the knife from the arm and to hold it in place on the grinding wheel or sharpening stone.) Smooth the rough edges on a grinder or with a file.

For the tool to work properly, it is critical that the knife be square to the surface of the arm but turned slightly away from parallel with the fence. Make practice runs on

Set the Knife

THE SLIGHT ANGLE IS CRITICAL to the tool's cutting action. The thin slot is laid out 3° or 4° off square, but it will be square vertically through the arm.

LAY OUT AND DRILL THE 1/4-IN.-DIA. RELIEF HOLE. With the center relieved and only the front and back of the slot to worry about, the blade will be easier to fit.

WHITTLE OUT THE TWO ENDS OF THE SLOT, fitting them to the blade. Only ⅛ in. of the blade should protrude from the bottom of the arm.

scrap stock until you get it down. Start by marking a 3- or 4-degree line on the arm, then drill a ¼-in.-dia. hole on that line. The hole and the slot that follows must be exactly perpendicular to the bottom face of the arm. Next, with a sharp knife, chisel, or thin keyhole saw, cut a notch just slightly thinner than the blade on each side of the hole, following the angled layout line and using the hole as a guide.

To tap the knife in, place the arm over a benchdog hole in your workbench so the blade tip can emerge below. The blade tip should protrude no more than ⅛ in. and be securely wedged.

Now and then your kebiki will need fine-tuning. Occasionally, you'll need to sharpen the blade. Eventually, you may have to replace the wedge as it wears, or at least give the edges that get the most wear a few licks with a plane or chisel. Otherwise it should serve you for many years. Like me, you will come to cherish this simple, useful, and elegant little tool.

* Please note price estimates are from 2001.

JOHN NESSET is a furniture maker in Minneapolis, Minnesota.

Sources

The Japan Woodworker
800-537-7820

Scratch Awl
from Scrap

BY TOM HEROLD

A scratch awl (or scribe) is an indispensable marking tool, which is capable of striking a finer and more useful line than you can get with a pencil. Beautiful versions of the tool are available commercially but often cost upward of $35★. For about a tenth of that, you can make one of your own. The tools you'll need are all fairly common: a woodworking lathe, a 3-jaw or 4-jaw chuck, a drill press, a grinder, and a standard propane torch. Once you've made your first scratch awl and you see how simple the process is, you'll make many more. Besides being fun to make, a scratch awl you've crafted yourself, which can't be matched by any tool you can buy, is satisfying to use.

Making a scratch awl is a great first project in metalworking, but you need to be aware of the hazards. When cutting metal on a wood lathe, remember to use eye protection, keep your hands and clothing out of the way and concentrate on the task.

Selecting Materials

Most of the awls I've made have been between 5 in. and 8 in. overall. I like to size my awls to take advantage of standard material sizes, most notably $3/16$-in.-dia. steel rod and $1/2$-in.-dia. brass rod, to minimize the amount of metalwork I have to do. For

the handles, I usually start with 1-in. stock, but sometimes the shaft's length seems to require a heftier handle, in which case I'll go with $1\frac{1}{2}$-in. stock.

For these awls, I used O-1 steel (a high-carbon, oil-hardening tool steel), which can be purchased through many industrial-supply companies. It costs only a few dollars a linear foot. I bought my brass at a scrap-metal yard for $2 a pound. I've also seen brass rod at home-improvement stores, but it's much more expensive. Making these awls also lets me use some of those beautiful scraps I can never throw away, and even if I buy handle stock, I can buy "shorts" from lumber dealers for very little and have the experience of working with an otherwise unaffordable exotic.

Working with Metal

Metalworking isn't that much different from working with wood; the material's just harder. I begin by hacksawing a piece of steel rod about 5 in. or 6 in. long and chucking it in my lathe's headstock, making sure the steel protrudes about $1/2$ in. Using the lathe's slowest speed, I file the end of

the steel smooth and flat to ready it for end drilling. Next I chuck a ¼-in. center drill (available from industrial-tool suppliers) into the tailstock of my lathe, squirt a bit of oil on the end of the steel rod and bore a hole in the end, just deep enough to seat the tailstock center, which will support the steel during turning.

Next, to prepare the brass collar, I cut a piece of ½-in.-dia. brass rod ½ in. long and chuck it in the headstock. The brass provides a nice transition from steel to wood. I clean up the end of the brass with a file and then use a skew to get the end flat where it will meet the wood. As with the steel, I use the lathe's slowest speed. After squirting a couple of drops of oil where I'm drilling to lubricate and cool the cut, I center drill the brass to the same diameter as the steel shaft.

I remove the brass from the lathe, clean it and the steel thoroughly with lacquer

SCRATCH AWLS CAN BE MADE in many sizes and shapes according to the kind of woodworking you do and your tastes. Here's a sampling of the author's collection.

thinner, and slide the steel through the brass. It's essential to remove all oil and dirt from both steel and brass; if you don't, you won't get a good solder joint. I leave enough steel on the handle side of the brass to form a tang, which will seat well in the handle. I leave enough steel on the other (center drilled) end for the shaft plus a little extra, which I'll cut off after tapering the shaft. I use a propane torch and regular pipe solder, making sure I get a good flow of solder on both sides of the brass. I don't worry about any excess solder now because I'll clean it up during the next operation.

I rechuck the brass in the headstock and support the center-drilled end of the shaft with the tailstock. Then I clean the solder joint with a metal file and shape the brass with a skew. Next I taper the steel shaft with a fine mill file, leaving just enough metal at the point for support—usually about $\frac{3}{32}$ in. thick. This seems to take forever, but it's really only about 10 minutes. I sand next, from about 220-grit down to 2,000-grit (very fine abrasive papers are available at most auto paint shops), which gives the shaft a nice finish.

I reverse the awl in the chuck (chucking the brass collar), so the tang is exposed. I clean the tang side with a file and skew just as I did the other side, making sure the brass is flat and perpendicular to the steel

rod, to ensure that the handle seats at the collar. I rough up the tang with a file to promote good adhesion and file a portion of it flat to ensure the handle won't rotate on the shaft.

Making the Handle

When picking wood for handle material, I look for interesting figure, dramatic color, or just plain beautiful wood. To prepare the handle blank for turning, I get one end flat and smooth, and then I drill a hole in the middle of that end deep enough for the tang and about $\frac{1}{32}$ in. larger in diameter. The extra space prevents the joint from being glue starved. After cleaning both steel and brass with lacquer thinner, I epoxy the handle to the shaft. If I can spare my lathe for 24 hours, I'll do it with the awl still in the chuck. Once the epoxy has cured, I turn the awl's handle to its final form.

I take it slowly when turning the handle. Although it's not easy to break the glue joint, it is possible. Sometimes I use the tailstock to keep the handle turning true until it's pretty much roughed out. Once the handle is close to the desired shape, I remove the brass collar from the chuck, back the awl out a bit and chuck the shaft. This gives me room to clean up the brass and get a good transition from the handle to the brass.

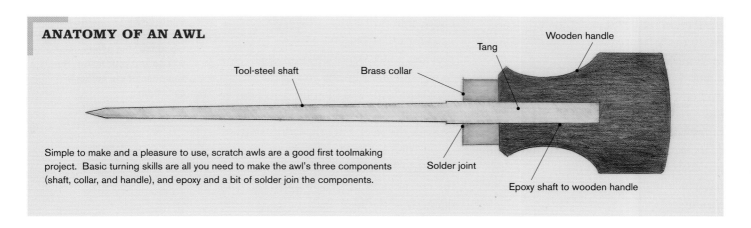

ANATOMY OF AN AWL

Tool-steel shaft

Brass collar

Tang

Wooden handle

Solder joint

Epoxy shaft to wooden handle

Simple to make and a pleasure to use, scratch awls are a good first toolmaking project. Basic turning skills are all you need to make the awl's three components (shaft, collar, and handle), and epoxy and a bit of solder join the components.

Once I'm satisfied with the handle's shape, I sand it smooth and finish it. I've used shellac, linseed oil, and Formby's® tung oil finish. It all depends on what look you like. My dad insists that the best finish for a wooden tool handle is just plain wax. I can't argue with that. With the handle finished, I take the awl out of the chuck, put the center-drilled end of the shaft in a vise, and, using a hacksaw, cut off the tip that extends beyond the taper.

Tempering and Sharpening the Shaft

The final steps in making the awl are tempering and sharpening the end of the shaft. Tempering is a two-stage process: hardening and drawing. To harden the steel, use your propane torch to heat the end of the awl to a cherry-red (or glowing red) color, just after it's gone through dull red. I hold the awl by its handle with one finger just touching the steel near the handle, and place the end of the shaft (back just a bit from the point) into the tip of the flame. As soon as the end of the shaft becomes cherry red (and before the shaft gets too hot to touch), I quickly place the shaft into a nearby can of motor oil.

Quenching the steel in oil like this will bring the temperature of the steel down rapidly, making it extremely hard and brittle—almost like glass. Because it's far too fragile for use at this point, I have to remove, or "draw," some of the brittleness from the steel by heating it up again. But this time I heat it only until it reaches a light straw color—about 430° Fahrenheit. Before I heat it up again, though, I clean up the shaft with very fine abrasive paper—1,000-grit—so I can see the color of the shaft when I do reheat it. Then I position the tip of the awl well above the flame and move the shaft in and out of the heat. Once the shaft starts to change color, the process goes very quickly. So carefully watch for the steel to start to take on the light straw color, and be prepared to plunge the blade into the motor oil immediately.

If all this talk of cherry red, dull red, and light straw sounds a bit daunting, don't worry. Temperature-indicator cards are available wherever welding supplies are sold. They show spectrums of color in correlation with temperatures and allow you to hazard a fairly accurate guess as to the temperature your steel has attained.

Finally, I sharpen the awl's shaft on a grinder. It's easy and virtually foolproof, just like sharpening a pencil on a belt sander. But then again, none of us have ever done that.

* Please note price estimates are from 1993.

TOM HEROLD is an aerospace engineer who works wood for pleasure. He lives in Colorado Springs, Colorado.

Story Sticks
Leave Little Room
for Error

BY MARIO RODRIGUEZ

If you asked a dozen woodworkers to measure and cut a piece of wood measuring 12 in., you'd likely end up with 12 pieces of slightly varying length. Each time a workpiece is measured and marked, an opportunity for error creeps into the process.

The error factor is an unavoidable aspect of human nature. We're not machines, and each time we repeat a task, the result is likely to be a little different than the time before. A momentary distraction or a tight deadline, and maybe you take a measurement from the wrong side of the piece, read the tape wrong, or simply forget a number. This results in a cabinet that doesn't fit into a designated space, a misplaced mortise on a cabinet frame, or turned legs that don't match.

The simplest way to ensure uniformity and accuracy is to eliminate some of that measuring, trading the by-the-numbers approach for direct transfer of dimensions. For years, woodworkers have used shop-made gauges called story sticks to create a physical record of a piece, not only improving their accuracy but also saving time.

A story stick is essentially a slender strip of wood (or metal) that holds a series of markings, notches, or notations designating the exact locations and profiles of critical elements. The stick can be used to produce multiples or be set aside to be reused in the future. The stick saves the time and trouble of remeasuring each time the information is needed, and it virtually eliminates measuring errors.

Story Sticks Are Invaluable for Cabinetry

These compact tools are especially useful on job sites for the layout and installation of architectural woodwork and cabinetry. But story sticks are also used by furniture makers, for chairs, turnings, or even case pieces.

I was introduced to story sticks as an apprentice working for a trim-carpentry company. When we installed kitchen cabinets and vanities in expensive New York high-rise apartments, we used story sticks to locate cutouts in the cabinets for electrical, water, and waste lines. The contractor wanted these holes located within ¼ in. of the pipes, so they had to be dead-on. After establishing a level line around the room, we placed a story stick either against the last-installed cabinet or the corner of the wall and marked the exact horizontal locations of pipes or outlets. Then, working from the same level line, we marked the vertical locations of the pipes on the other side of the stick. Thus we were able to record confidently the locations of the cutouts without suffering the gut-wrenching fear that we might tear a hole through the back of a custom cabinet and be 2 in. off the mark.

Story sticks are also used to lay out entire kitchens. The horizontal and vertical positions of each unit can be planned and recorded on a length of narrow plywood. Aside from the other benefits, a story stick serves as a double-check for blueprint dimensions. Sometimes planning and design

errors that were missed on the blueprints are caught when the actual kitchen is laid out on the stick.

A story stick is also useful for the installation of hinges and drawer slides on a cabinet carcase.

The Chairmaker's Story Stick

For makers of ladder backs and other post-and-rung chairs, a story stick is indispensable, holding everything the maker needs to reproduce a chair. No drawings are necessary. The surface of the stick will bear the decorative profile, center, and diameter of each mortise and dimensions of each tenon. It allows the craftsman to mark the decorative divisions and precisely locate any mortises along the leg. Often a chairmaker's

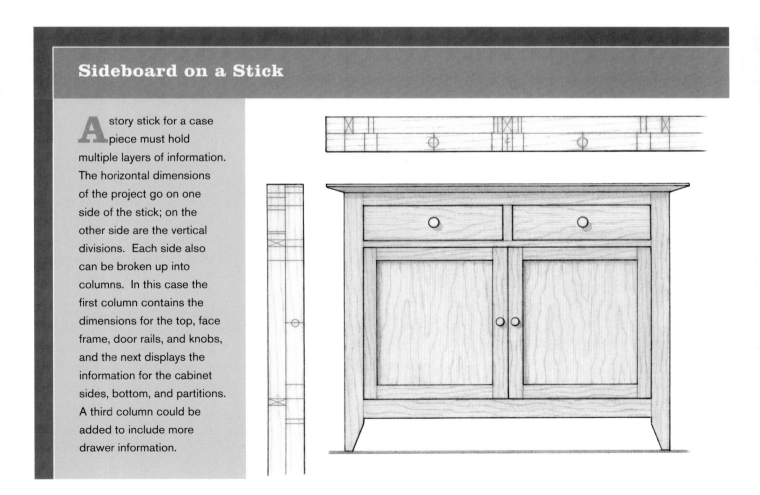

Sideboard on a Stick

A story stick for a case piece must hold multiple layers of information. The horizontal dimensions of the project go on one side of the stick; on the other side are the vertical divisions. Each side also can be broken up into columns. In this case the first column contains the dimensions for the top, face frame, door rails, and knobs, and the next displays the information for the cabinet sides, bottom, and partitions. A third column could be added to include more drawer information.

stick will have a small hook on one end for quick and accurate registration at the end of the leg.

Furniture Makers Also Benefit

For years I used story sticks in the shop when building furniture and freestanding cabinets. Sometimes I laid out the sticks from scaled blueprints; other times I made them from full-size drawings. You may have a favorite piece that you find yourself building again and again. A story stick can hold everything you need to jog your memory.

Why prepare a story stick when there are drawings? Well, sometimes the information necessary to build the piece is contained on more than one sheet. This requires unfurling, flipping, and cross-checking. Usually a single story stick can contain all of the critical measurements. The horizontal divisions and features of the project go on one side of the stick; on the other side of the stick are the vertical divisions.

Drawings get dirty, torn, or wet in a normal shop environment. Story sticks are more durable. In my shop we cut the dimensions into the stick with a marking knife, darken them with a pencil, then seal the stick with a coat of lacquer; or we use indelible markers. To distinguish the sticks quickly from the countless other plywood scraps lying about, we highlight them with bright spray paint.

One of the best things about a story stick is that it can be used to set up a machine quickly and accurately. The story stick for a cabinet, for example, can be placed directly on the table saw to set the fence for ripping or to place a stop block for crosscutting. By the way, storing a stick is easy: Drill a ½-in.-dia. hole at one end and hang it on the wall.

There tends to be more information on a furniture story stick than on a cabinet-installation stick, so I divide a furniture stick into columns. Each column is for a different layer of the project. If one column contains the dimensions for the face frame and door rails, the next displays the information for the cabinet sides, bottom, rails and partitions, and the last contains dimensions for the drawer box. As you read the stick from left to right, the information takes you deeper into the cabinet.

Turners Use Them Too

When building Windsor chairs, I often have to turn 40 or 50 legs at a time. I've preserved my sanity by developing a smooth routine, which starts with a story stick. Turners almost always work from a story stick, whether it's an actual strip of wood or just a strip of masking tape on the tool rest. My basic story stick is a scrap of plywood with a profile of the leg drawn onto it. Lines through the important divisions of the turning are extended to the edge of the stick and are used to mark the blank as it spins on the lathe.

A snazzier version is another strip of ½-in.-thick plywood with the pattern drawn onto it, but this one has 4d nails protruding at the significant divisions. Once the leg blank is round, I press the stick against the spinning workpiece and scribe every critical dimension in one shot. With the aid of the story stick, it takes me about three minutes to turn a leg.

Many woodworkers aren't aware of story sticks, which are part of the age-old practice of direct layout. Why measure twice to cut once when you can be sure the first time?

MARIO RODRIGUEZ is a contributing editor to *Fine Woodworking* magazine and the author of *Building Fireplace Mantels* (Taunton Press, 2002).

THE TURNER'S STORY STICK. Rodriguez made this stick for the front leg of a 17th-century corner chair. Each mark represents an important transition point. Spindle turning often begins with a parting tool plunging in to establish the depths at these key points. Then the turner works to reproduce the finished profile.

Three Everyday Chisels

BY SVEN HANSON

The number-one cleanup device in my shop isn't a broom or a vacuum, as any visitor can tell you. It's a chisel. Every ragged rabbet, gloppy glueline or oversize tenon can be improved by the touch of a sharp chisel. When fine joinery is required, it's a sure thing chisels will be part of creating the perfect fit. You need chisels to chop out hand-cut dovetails, to square the corners of router-cut rabbets, and to trim countersunk plugs.

The bench chisel family tree has three main branches: bevel-edge chisels for a variety of trimming and paring work, mortise chisels for serious chopping, and the catchall category of firmer chisels for light-duty mortising or heavy-duty paring (see the photo above).

There are other, more specialized types of chisels, but your workshop will be well-equipped if you carefully choose a few chisels from each of the three main groups.

85

BEVEL-EDGE CHISEL–CLEANING OUT A DOVETAIL. Beveled sides allow a dovetail chisel to squeeze into tight quarters.

of weights and shapes, give you the most control and are friendly to a chisel's handle.

Choose the Chisels for Your Shop

I have collected a pretty full set of each style of chisel, but they're not all necessary.

Bevel-edge chisels, so called because they have three bevels on their faces, fit easily inside dadoes and dovetails. I use my ½-in. and ¾-in. chisels all the time and chop out dovetails with ⅜-in., ½-in., or ⅝-in. chisels.

When picking out mortising chisels, select ones based on the size mortises you plan to chop. These are costly; there's no value in owning a whole set if you routinely chop out only ¼-in. mortises. I find ⅛-in., ¼-in., ⅜-in., and ½-in. mortise chisels serve most of my needs.

My firmer chisels play the utility in-fielder position, doing the work that might damage a thin-blade bevel-edge chisel or chopping small mortises on more delicate projects. You might need a few, ranging in size from ¼ in. to ¾ in.

Bevel-Edge Chisels Are Used in Tight Quarters

Along one leg of my Bermuda work triangle formed by bench, table saw, and jointer I've mounted a kitchen-style magnetic knife holder. It holds a handful of bevel-edge chisels, which I use more frequently than either my firmer or mortise chisels.

Bevel-edge chisels are sometimes called paring chisels, and there are two subcategories. Short, sturdy paring chisels are called butt or carpenter's chisels, and long-blade ones are known as dovetail chisels.

Butt chisels get into tight quarters You'll find some version of the short, sturdy chisel in every carpenter's tool belt. You don't need a long, delicate chisel for chopping out a ⅛-in.-deep door hinge mortise. And if you're working inside a cabinet, the short butt chisel allows you room enough to

The main thing to consider when shopping for chisels is your needs. If you plan to do a lot of heavy chopping in hardwoods, the money invested in tools with reinforced handles and properly tempered steel will be well worth it. But if you use chisels infrequently or if you use them for light-duty work, you could get by with moderately priced tools. And if you need chisels to do some rough work, like chopping away at interior trim where there's the likelihood of hitting nails, buy inexpensive chisels.

Chisels demand proper striking tools. Handles with metal striking caps or ferrules at both ends can be whacked with a hammer; unreinforced handles require a mallet. Wooden mallets, which come in a variety swing a hammer without striking the other side of the case. This chisel is easy to hold and maneuver across a glued-up panel when scraping squeeze-out.

Dovetail chisels have long blades A dovetail chisel's long blade makes it easier to see your work and gauge whether you're holding the tool perpendicular to the workpiece. Dovetail chisels have blades that are sharply beveled on the sides to allow you to work right into the triangular bottom of a dovetail joint (see the photo on the facing page).

I rely on countersunk and plugged screws to hold a lot of things together. Dovetail chisels are great for paring off the screw plug flush to the frame, because I can approach the cut with the long blade nearly flat on the wood. I take a careful trial cut across the top of the plug to find the paring direction that goes with the grain. I take roughly 1/16-in. slices off the plug to pare it flush to the surrounding surface. It's not as fast as belt sanding, but if done carefully you get better results with less noise and less risk to the surrounding surface.

Firmer Chisels Look Like Skinny Mortise Chisels

The firmer chisel is a compromise tool that is often too light for heavy-duty mortising but too thick to work inside the confines of furniture joints. This chisel is also called a sash mortise chisel, named by American makers of window sashes, or a registered mortise chisel. Firmer chisels have only one bevel on the face, like mortise chisels, and the blades are thinner than they are wide.

I own a set of ash-handled Greenlee® firmers. They reside in their own drawer away from the squalor of everyday working-class tools. As a result, they're usually the sharpest of the bunch. These chisels come in handy when you have to pare down a tight tenon (see the photo below). For good control when taking off a thin shaving, you can use their square sides to ride along the tenon's shoulder.

If you want to do some serious chopping, the double-hooped handle with leather shock ring at the blade's shoulder can take a hard shot with a 22-oz. framing hammer. The only maintenance besides

FIRMER CHISEL–PARING A TIGHT TENON. **Instead of heading back to the table saw to narrow a tenon, use a razor-sharp firmer chisel. Its square edge rides along a tenon's shoulder and makes paper-thin shavings.**

sharpening is grinding off the mushroom edge that forms on the hoop that protects the butt end from splitting. I round it back by rolling the edge against the belt sander.

Mortise Chisels Need to Be Strong

Mortise chisels are the big brutes of the chisel world. They have rectangular blades that can be thicker than they are wide. You need this heft when prying out a chip that's wedged deep inside a mortise.

Quality mortise chisels have a very hefty tang, a steel extension of the blade that fits up into the handle. The sturdiest have reinforcing ferrules, also called hoops, at the tang and at the butt of the handle to prevent splitting when the chisel is struck with a hammer or mallet. If a mortising chisel does not have a ferrule at the striking end of the handle, it's meant to be used with a nonmetal mallet.

To reduce the chance of splitting a workpiece when chopping mortises, I clamp a hand screw to the sides of the stock where the waste will be removed (see the photo at left). A second clamp holds the whole piece firmly to the workbench. Besides preventing splitting, this clamp system lets you cut faster and with more control while keeping chips from creeping under the workpiece and dinging it.

Anatomy of Chisels

There are two main components to chisels: the steel and the handle. Determining what kind of steel and how well a tool has been tempered can't be done by eye. You can get an idea about the strength of the handle by looking for reinforcing ferrules or striking caps and examining how it's fastened to the steel, whether by a socket (strongest) or a skinny tang (weakest).

I'm not obsessed with finding just the right hardness rating for my chisels. If you order tools from big mail-order outlets, you can usually find out about the type of tool steel and hardness of the chisels they carry. But if you pick up a set at the local hardware store, that information may not be available to you.

Michael Burke, technical advisor at Garrett Wade, a mail-order tool supplier, told me that "most chisels range around Rc58 to Rc61 (Rockwell C hardness scale) with Japanese chisels running about three points higher. The precise hardness doesn't really matter because a difference of a point or two is like the difference between 600-grit and 700-grit sandpaper."

I have noticed that the most inexpensive chisels on the market are often on the soft side, although I have seen a few that were quite hard and brittle. Hardness is both a function of the metal's carbon content (and other additives) and how the tool was hardened and tempered.

Good tool steel has enough additives to allow hardening, which is accomplished by heating the metal to cherry red and then quickly cooling the tool. It is then reheated to a lower temperature, which reduces or tempers the hardness, making it less brittle and easier to sharpen. A chisel with a very hard tip is prone to chipping.

Conversely, poor steel that has not been hardened properly or steel that has been tempered too soft will bend at the thin cutting edge when pounded into hardwood. It will, however, be easy to grind and sharpen. Toolmakers aim for a balance between these two qualities.

Good steel, quality control in hardening and tempering, and strong handles add to the price of a chisel. Medium- and high-quality chisels will cost about $10 to $30★, sometimes more, apiece.

Sockets are found on the best chisels

Top-of-the-line older chisels were hand-forged with sockets. The blacksmith would pound one end of the metal around an anvil and create a conical section for the handle to fit inside. Modern socket chisels have their sockets machine-forged or welded on.

Sockets are available on all three types of chisels. When you strike a socket chisel, the wooden handle compresses into the tapered socket, which keeps everything firmly united.

Look for a sturdy handle

The handle, not the blade, is the Achilles heel of most chisels. When chopping mortises, all the force of a hard-swung mallet strikes a spot that's 1 in. in diameter or less. Chisel handles made of wood come with and without reinforcing ferrules, which increase their strength. A lot of chisels are made with plastic handles, and I've found these to be very sturdy even though they don't have the traditional look and warm feel of wood. If you plan to use a hammer to strike them, buy ones with metal striking caps.

Wood tends to split if struck hard. To counter that, the makers of wooden tool handles taper them. The small-diameter end helps center the mallet's blow to the tool and reduces splitting. Toolmakers often add metal ferrules to the handle to keep the wood fibers squeezed tightly together. If the grain is straight and you avoid metal hammers, single-ferrule chisels are durable enough.

Many craftspeople prefer a heftier handle. A chisel handle made of wood with ferrules at both ends can take a lot of force. These chisels can be used with metal hammers or large mallets.

There's another way to strengthen a handle. Some chisels are made with a thick leather washer pressed over a tenon round left projecting from the end of the turned handle. This evens the blow around the edge of the handle and prevents splitting. These are medium-duty chisels meant to be used by hand or with a light mallet.

Mallets Deliver a Little or a Lot of Power

You can use a hammer when striking chisels, but it's best to use a wooden or hard plastic mallet. They're much kinder on handles. Mallets, with their large faces, also make it easier to deliver the force of the blow to the chisel instead of, say, the hand holding the chisel. Good mallets run from $12 to $50.

Mallets come in various weights. I find that 16-oz. to 22-oz. mallets are suitable for chopping dovetails. For heavier work, such as chopping mortises, 22-oz. to 32-oz. mallets work well. There are some woodworkers who favor 3-lb. mallets, but it certainly takes a lot of strength to handle one of these behemoths for hours on end.

Mallets also come in different shapes. The big square mallets, called joiner's mallets, are usually the heaviest of the bunch and great for use with mortise chisels. For

Angling for Precision Cuts

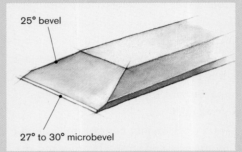

Not all bevels are created equal. If you cut hardwoods, a steeper bevel on your chisel will stay sharp longer. If you cut softwoods, you will need a shallow bevel angle to shear the wood fibers, not crush them. I use secondary, or microbevels, on all my chisels. The bevel-edge and firmer chisels get a very short microbevel at the cutting edge, which is created when I'm doing my final honing on a superfine stone. I lift the chisel up just slightly to create that microbevel. That way, when I resharpen, I only have to hone a very narrow edge, not the entire bevel.

For softwoods, a microbevel of 27 degrees or so allows easier entry into the wood (see the drawing at right). For hardwoods, a microbevel of 30 degrees to 35 degrees cuts cleanly enough and stays sharp longer than a more acute bevel. If you plan to do a lot of hand-paring, you'll want microbevels in the 27-degree to 30-degree range. But if you plan to use a heavy mallet, microbevels of 30 degrees or more will hold an edge longer.

For fine work on delicate projects no matter what the wood, I use a 27-degree to 30-degree microbevel, especially when using the chisel without a mallet. This angle decreases the force necessary to cut. I pay for it with more frequent sharpening.

I modify the bevels on my mortise chisels by grinding the long bevel about 28 degrees and honing a secondary bevel of about 35 degrees to 40 degrees at the tip (see the drawing at right). The long bevel permits easy passage of the chisel body into the nether regions of a cut. The blunt tip leaves more metal where it counts.

Sharpening Angles for Bevel-Edge and Firmer Chisels

25° bevel

27° to 30° microbevel

For chiseling softwoods or hand-paring, grind a shallow microbevel of 27 degrees to 30 degrees. When working in hardwoods, a tip ground 30 degrees to 35 degrees will hold up longer.

Regrind Mortise Chisels with a Long Bevel

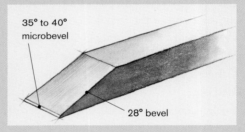

35° to 40° microbevel

28° bevel

tight quarters or for chopping at odd angles, a round carver's mallet works well. You can also use a rubber mallet or a dead-blow hammer.

Safety Glasses Protect Your Eyes from Flying Chips

Experience has taught me three rules for safe chisel use. First, keep all your body parts behind the tip of the chisel, well out of its path. Second, clamp down the workpiece unless it's so heavy that it won't move while chopping. Third, always wear safety glasses. Ordinary eyeglasses will do for par-

ing on the benchtop, but when I use a hammer or work overhead, I'm partial to goggles.

One time, when I took a chisel to the underside of a teak handrail while wearing ordinary eyeglasses—not safety glasses—a tiny boulder rolled past my glasses into my eye, and it stuck. I learned my lesson.

* Please note price estimates are from 1997.

SVEN HANSON builds custom furniture in Albuquerque, New Mexico.

Japanese Chisels

BY WILLIAM TANDY YOUNG

JAPANESE CHISELS HAVE A CON-CAVE BACK, which makes them easier to flatten. Regular flattening prevents the hollow from reaching the cutting edge.

I have a passion for chisels. But when I first encountered Japanese chisels, I wasn't interested in them, despite the rave reviews. They were expensive and up-keep seemed too bothersome. Besides, how superior could they be to my Western chisels?

I eventually gave in to my curiosity about Japanese chisels and tried a few of them (see the photo above). For once, the tool hype is true: The laminated steel blade of a Japanese chisel takes and holds an astounding edge. The distinctive hollow in the back of the chisel reduces its surface area, which makes it easy to flatten the tool quickly and precisely.

Japanese chisels are compact and hefty. They're ideal for striking with a hammer,

Handle Preparation

REMOVE THE FACTORY COATING from blade and handle. Soak new chisels in lacquer thinner.

HAMMER THE HOOP SQUARELY on the handle using a slightly larger hoop as a driving ring.

CAREFULLY MUSHROOM THE END. Using a household iron, the author steams the handle butt. With glancing hammer blows, he peens the end as he rotates the chisel.

COMPLETED HANDLE BUTT. After peening, the end of the handle should be a neat, shallow dome that feels comfortable in your palm.

and they allow you to keep your hands close to the work. They have a comfortable, balanced feel and offer superb control. Japanese chisels raise trimming and chopping to a more refined, intimate level.

Now I work regularly with both Western and Japanese chisels, and I wouldn't want to be without either. By adding Japanese chisels to your tool kit, you can bring hand-tool performance to a new level. One word of warning, though: If you choose unsuitable Japanese chisels or you prepare them poorly, you will be disappointed.

Shop-Worthy Chisels

Though Japan is famous for high-quality goods, it also produces lots of cheap, inferior merchandise—chisels included. I have a few low-quality Japanese chisels that are brittle and unpleasant to work with. I wouldn't recommend them to anyone at any skill level. Even if you're just starting out, try to get decent chisels so that you'll always enjoy using them, no matter how experienced you become.

Quality can be a hard thing to figure, though. From rare and exotic to common and cheap, Japanese tool quality is wide-ranging. It's hard to keep track of all the various names, steels, forging methods, and toolmakers' reputations.

Japanese wholesalers and exporters add to the confusion by routinely changing the brand names of tools. The same Japanese chisel might be sold under several different labels in the West. That's why it's best to buy Japanese chisels from knowledgeable specialty dealers (see sources). Get their help in matching a good-quality tool to your skill level and the type of work you do. Large Western tool retailers that sell Japanese tools as a sideline may not know much about them.

You also can ask woodworkers experienced with Japanese chisels for their suggestions. The ones I talked with steered me away from both the cheap chisels and the most expensive ones. They suggested basic, professional-grade chisels, made of durable, good-quality steel and plain oak handles, and common blade shapes. These everyday chisels, called oire-nomi, are great all-purpose tools, excelling at everything from musical-instrument making to timber-frame carpentry. They stand up to rugged use better than many of the more precious Japanese chisels that have ebony handles and ink-patterned, hand-hammered blades.

The first time that I ordered some oire-nomi chisels (expect to pay from $15★ to more than $25 apiece for decent ones), there was a handwritten note at the bottom of the invoice that said, "These are simple, but tough." I knew I had bought the right ones.

Getting a Japanese Chisel Ready for Use

Like many hand tools, Japanese chisels usually aren't ready to use right out of the package. Before I began tuning up my chisels for the first time, I sifted through all the advice that I had read or heard and then worked out the methods that follow. They may not be traditional, but these methods will help you get the best performance from your chisels.

Remove the coating The first thing to do with new Japanese chisels is strip off the thick, protective coating. Soak the chisels in a container of lacquer thinner for a half hour or so (see the top left photo on the facing page). Remove each chisel, and slip the metal hoop off the top of the handle. Wipe the residue from the hoops and tools with thinner and a rag. Use a respirator and gloves, and exhaust the fumes while you do this.

Seat the handle hoop After the coating has been stripped off, the hoops need to be driven onto the handles to seat them firmly in place. Japanese chisels usually are struck with a steel hammer for chopping cuts. A

Grind and Hone the Bevel

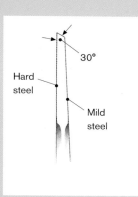

GRIND THE BEVEL TO 30 DEGREES. **Use a jig and a flat waterstone grinder or a disc sander.**

30°

Hard steel

Mild steel

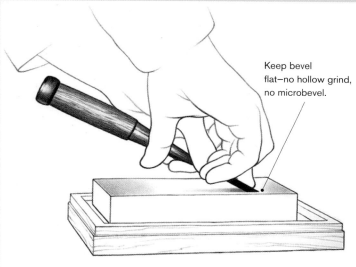

Keep bevel flat—no hollow grind, no microbevel.

Once the bevel is reestablished, hone the bevel on progressively finer waterstones. Keep pressure more toward the tip where the harder steel of the blade is.

well-seated hoop prevents the chisel handle from splitting under such pounding. If any of the hoops have ridges or burrs on the inside that would prevent them from seating properly, file them smooth first.

Sources

**Aqua Sharpening
Stone and Tool, Inc.**
819 Stannage Ave.
Albany, CA 94706
(510) 525-8948

**Hida Tool
and Hardware**
1333 San Pablo Ave.
Berkeley, CA 94702
(510) 524-3700

**The Japan
Woodworker**
1731 Clement Ave.
Alameda, CA 94501
(800) 537-7820

The handles and hoops are paired in graduated sizes to correspond with blade widths. If you start with your smallest chisel, you can use the hoop from one of the larger chisels as a driving ring to seat the smaller hoop. You could also use a piece of pipe or an electrical coupling. With the tip of the blade pushed into a scrap block on the benchtop, hammer the hoops onto the handles (see the top right photo on p. 92). Seat the hoops so the handle protrudes about 1/16 in. If a hoop won't seat down on the handle that far, pull it off and sand or scrape the handle slightly. If a hoop seats too far down the handle, carefully sand the excess handle end.

Peen over the butt Once the hoops are seated, I secure them by peening over the handle ends. This can be tedious, but the tool handles will be more durable and pleasant to grip. The end grain of each handle has to be softened so that you can hammer it into a dome. Dab the handle end lightly with water (don't submerge the hoop), and then touch it on a heated, inverted clothes iron for a few seconds. The heat and steam will soften the fibers.

Jam the blade back into your wood scrap on the benchtop and then start mushrooming the handle end evenly with light blows of a framing hammer (see the middle photo on p. 92). Rotate the chisel as you go, and try to draw the wood from the center of the handle out to the edge with each stroke. Reheat the end of the handle often so that you can shape it neatly into a dome (see the bottom photo on p. 92) without mashing it into a pulpy mess. Let the peened-over ends dry out and then give the handles two or three coats of Waterlox® or Behlen's Salad Bowl oil.

Reshape the bevel Most Japanese chisels have a bevel angle that's too low for kiln-dried hardwoods (about 25 degrees). Reestablish the angle to about 30 degrees (see the photo on p. 93). The exact bevel angle depends on the chisel and the kind of work that you do. The best guide is to raise the bevel angle until the edge no longer nicks or crumbles as you work.

When you are changing the bevel angle, remember that Japanese chisels work best when the bevel is kept full and flat. Don't hollow grind the bevel, hone a microbevel, or use other typical Western tool-sharpening methods. The Japanese chisel blade is a sophisticated sandwich of hard and mild steel. The hard, delicate edge steel on the back of the blade needs the full support of the mild steel behind it for durability.

Hone the edge After shaping the bevel, hone it on waterstones. I don't use a honing jig because some blade shapes aren't suitable for jigs. Instead, I use a two-hand grip (see the drawing on p. 93). With practice, it's not that hard to keep the ample bevel of a thick Japanese chisel blade riding flat on a sharpening stone. It's also not tedious because Japanese waterstones cut fast. I begin with a fairly coarse stone and quickly proceed through progressively finer grits. While honing, focus pressure toward the tip of the blade. (Waterstones abrade the mild steel at the rear of the bevel faster than the hard steel at the tip.)

Dress the blade back You have to flatten the back of a Japanese chisel blade before you use it. And you should re-dress the back from time to time to maintain a cutting edge. Before flattening, check the back of the shaft above the blade. It should be flush with the back or slightly shy of it.

The shaft often is left proud by the maker. This hinders the accurate flattening of the blade back and restricts the range of the chisel. If the back of the shaft is proud, relieve it until it is barely shy of the blade back (see the top left drawing on the facing page). You can use a power waterstone wheel, a bench grinder, or a 1-in.-wide belt sander, but don't touch the blade area itself.

RELIEVE THE SHANK AND FLATTEN THE BACK

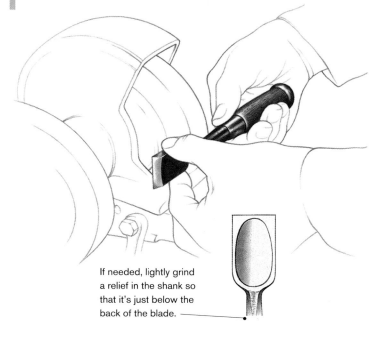

If needed, lightly grind a relief in the shank so that it's just below the back of the blade.

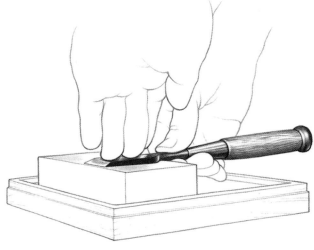

Flatten the back on waterstones, working the blade at a right angle to the length of the stone. Start with coarse stones (220 or 400), and then follow with finer ones (700 and higher).

New Chisel

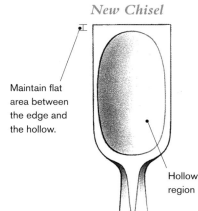

Maintain flat area between the edge and the hollow.

Hollow region

Slightly Used Chisel

Worn Chisel

The back of a Japanese chisel should be flattened initially and redressed periodically. Each time the back is flattened, the thickness of the blade is reduced, so the hollow shrinks and never reaches the cutting edge.

Relieving the shank slightly will not weaken the tool.

Hone the back of the blade until it's flat, starting with a coarse waterstone (220 grit or 400 grit), followed by finer stones (see the top right drawing). Rub the back on stones until the blade has an even, polished appearance overall.

Make sure that the hollow is encircled by a continuous rim of honed steel. This is critical at the tip of the blade, where repeated sharpening or bevel reshaping can cause the back of the cutting edge to recede into the hollow area. If this happens, hone vigorously, beginning with your coarsest stone, until you reestablish a complete, flat rim of steel around the hollow (see the bottom drawing).

Once both sides of the blade are honed and brightly polished, lightly oil the blade with camellia oil or mineral oil.

* Please note price estimates are from 1995.

WILLIAM TANDY YOUNG is a furniture maker and conservator in Stow, Massachusetts.

Choosing and Using Japanese Handsaws

BY TOSHIO ODATE

TRADITIONAL JAPANESE HANDSAWS COME IN MANY STYLES to suit different cutting situations, but all cut on the pull stroke. The saws, or noko, displayed in front of Odate are (from left to right) Anahiki-noko (log saw), ryoba-noko (combined rip and crosscut saw), azebiki-noko (for cuts in the center of a panel), kataba-noko (rip saw), dozuki-noko (fine crosscut saw), and kugihiki-noko (flush trimming saw).

I remember the first time I went to Atlanta, Georgia, to lecture on Japanese woodworking tools. I packed most of my tools in my luggage except my saws. I kept them with me because they were fragile. But when I tried to carry them through the gate to the airplane, I was surrounded by security guards. They did not believe me right away when I explained that the peculiar-looking saws I carried were actually woodworking tools.

Perhaps it was the exotic appearance of Japanese saws that first caught the eyes of many Western woodworkers when these tools became popular in America around the early 1970s. But even though the Japanese planes and chisels that appeared around that time gained rapid acceptance, many Westerners who first bought the saws were disappointed with the results. That isn't surprising, because these saws are very different from their Western counterparts. Also, there wasn't a lot of information available at that time about how Japanese saws should be used.

I will describe several Japanese saws that are most useful to cabinetmakers, including more general-purpose saws, like the ryoba-, kataba-, and dozuki-nokogiri (nokogiri or just noko means saw in Japanese), as well as more specialized saws, such as the azebiki- and kugihiki-nokogiri (see the photo on the facing page). I'll also describe how to properly take a cut with each one.

Japanese Saw Design

Unlike Western saws, which cut on the push stroke, Japanese saws all cut on the pull stroke. Sawing with a pulling action allows you to cut using both arms and the muscles of the entire body, without having to put your body weight into the stroke. This suited the traditional Japanese shokunin (craftsman), who typically worked in a squatting or sitting position. Because a Japanese saw is put into tension during cutting, the blade can be made very thin and

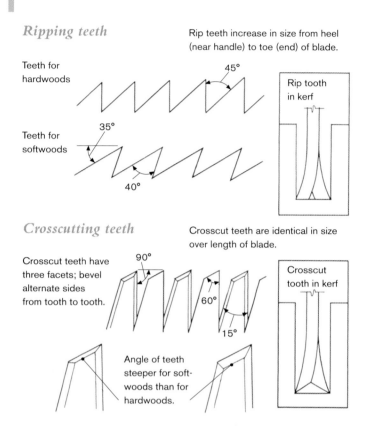

Ripping teeth

Rip teeth increase in size from heel (near handle) to toe (end) of blade.

Teeth for hardwoods

45°

Rip tooth in kerf

Teeth for softwoods

35°

40°

Crosscutting teeth

Crosscut teeth are identical in size over length of blade.

Crosscut teeth have three facets; bevel alternate sides from tooth to tooth.

90°

Crosscut tooth in kerf

60°

15°

Angle of teeth steeper for softwoods than for hardwoods.

from harder steel, so teeth stay sharp longer. Furthermore, a thin blade removes less material, so it requires less power to use.

The teeth on Japanese saws work on the same principle as their Western counterparts but have some important differences. Rip teeth are graduated, so they're smaller at the blade's heel (near the handle) and larger at the toe (see the drawing above). Crosscut teeth remain the same size along the length of the blade but have an extra bevel on top. The angle of the teeth and the top bevel of crosscut teeth also vary, depending on whether the saw is made for cutting hardwoods or softwoods.

Ryoba-Nokogiri

This is the Japanese saw most commonly known in the West. It has rip teeth on one edge and crosscut teeth on the other. The blade is narrower at the heel than at the toe and slightly thinner in the center than at the edges to decrease binding in the kerf. Ryoba-noko are available in many sizes, with blades ranging from 8 in. to 14 in. long. The number of teeth per inch depends on blade length; the smaller saws have finer teeth than the larger ones. A small ryoba-noko would be used by a craftsman for fine cutting jobs, such as mitering trim for installing cabinets or framing doors. The larger saws are often used by carpenters and are especially good for cutting large tenons for a timber-frame house.

USING TWO HANDS ON THE RYOBA-NOKO yields maximum power and control. Here the author cuts a tenon's shoulder using the saw's crosscutting teeth. He'll flip the saw over and use the rip teeth on the other edge for cutting the tenon's cheeks.

Ryoba-noko are typically used with both hands, although small saws can be used one handed. When using two hands, space them well apart for maximum power and control, as shown in the photo below. To start a cut, use the fingernail of your left index finger or thumb as a guide (if you are a lefty, use the other hand). Start your cut near the heel of the blade where the rip teeth are smaller and hold the blade at a 30-degree to 40-degree angle up from the surface of the workpiece. Once the cut is started, you can raise the angle of the blade. Keep in mind that the greater the angle of the saw to the work, the easier the cut—the smaller the angle, the better your control. When cutting wood between ¼ in. and ½ in. thick, use a shallower saw angle to decrease the tendency of the wood to vibrate as you cut. You don't have to apply very much down pressure (especially on the push return stroke when the teeth aren't cutting) for the saw to cut properly. If you're ripping a long board or panel, you may spread the kerf slightly with small wooden wedges to decrease binding and to prevent the saw teeth from scratching the cut surfaces.

The kataba-noko is a variation of the ryoba-noko. It has either ripping or cross-cutting teeth on only one edge. By not passing an extra set of teeth through the kerf of a thick workpiece, as the ryoba-noko does, the kataba-noko allows smoother cut surfaces. Kataba-noko are available in a size range similar to ryoba-noko.

Dozuki-Nokogiri

The dozuki-noko is a kataba-style crosscut saw with an extremely thin blade supported with a rigid strip of steel or brass folded over its back edge. It is commonly used to cut tenon shoulders on small members, as shown in the photo on p. 99 (tenon shoulders are called dozuki, giving the saw its name). Dozuki-noko have blades that range from 8 in. to 11 in. long. The smallest saw has 28 teeth per inch, the largest has 17 tpi.

THE RIGID-BACKED DOZUKI-NOKO makes fine crosscuts with small teeth that leave a very smooth cut surface. It's a good choice for cutting tenon cheeks, as shown here, or for other joinery.

Like any other crosscut saw, the dozuki-noko's teeth are the same size from heel to toe and have very little set, which results in a cut so smooth that neither a chisel nor a plane is required for finishing. The bevel ground on the top of the teeth varies depending upon whether the saw is to be used with hardwood or softwood (see the drawing on p. 97)

Dozuki-nokos are usually used one handed, but every craftsman has a different grip. Most of the time I hold the last third of the handle, but sometimes I hold the front third. It depends on the work. I stretch the index finger of my right hand along the top of the handle and press down gently while sawing. Start your cut just as with a ryoba-noko, using the nail of your left index finger or thumb as a guide. Cut

at first with the teeth near the toe of the saw, holding the blade at a 10-degree to 15-degree angle to the work. Use only the front third of the blade and cut with short strokes until you have cut about ³⁄₁₆ in. into the workpiece. Gradually lengthen your strokes until you are using the full length of the blade, keeping the blade parallel to the surface of the wood. Try to keep your strokes as straight as possible, as even small deviations can result in a kinked blade or broken teeth. A crooked stroke can also cause the saw to bind in the kerf. To make the cutting action smoother and discourage rust from developing, wipe the sawblade with a little Camellia oil (available from The Japan Woodworker; see Sources on p. 100) or vegetable oil.

Sources

Japanese saws can be mail ordered from the following companies.

Hida Inc.
1333 San Pablo Ave.
Berkeley, CA 94702
(800) 443-5512

The Japan Woodworker
1731 Clement Ave.
Alameda, CA 94501
(800) 537-7820

Nippon-4-Less
5477 Sharon Lane
San Jose, CA 95124
(408) 356-4184

Tashiro's
2939 Fourth Ave. S.
#101
Seattle, WA 98134
(206) 621-0199

THE AZEBIKI-NOKO CAN START A CUT in the middle of any surface, allowing it to do cutouts or stopped grooves. The author uses a straight stick to guide the saw while cutting the sides of a slot, which will be chiseled out later.

Azebiki-Nokogiri

The azebiki-noko is a ryoba-style saw, with crosscut and rip teeth on its short, curved blade and a long neck that fits into the handle. The curved cutting edge allows you to begin a cut in the center of a board, perfect for making stopped cuts or dadoes in a carcase panel (see the photo above). The azebiki-noko is also useful for sawing sliding-dovetail joints (a dozuki-noko could also be used, but long cuts that build up sawdust in the kerf can clog a dozuki's fine teeth). Azebiki-noko are also available in the kataba style (teeth only on one edge) with an offset neck that allows your hands to clear the wood more easily than with the ryoba-style saw.

Kugihiki-Nokogiri

This kataba-style crosscut saw looks like a dozuki without the back support. It has a blade about 7 in. long and is mainly used to flush trim through tenons or dowels (traditionally, the kugihiki-noko was used to cut wooden nails used to join softwood parts, hence kugihiki means to cut nails). The number of teeth per inch varies from 20 to 26 depending on the fineness of the work the saw is intended for. The body of a kugihiki-noko is quite thick near the handle and thin at the end. This allows the saw to bend easily. During cutting, the front two-thirds of the blade is held flat against the work, as shown in the photo on the facing page. Because the kugihiki-noko's teeth have no set, the cut part's surface is very smooth and no scratches are left on the wood surrounding it.

A KUGIHIKI-NOKO CAN FLUSH TRIM A DOWEL and leave behind a smoothly cut surface that needs no further sanding. Its teeth have no set, so they won't scratch the surrounding panel.

Saws with Changeable Blades

Traditional Japanese saws are difficult to sharpen. A convenient alternative is a saw with a changeable, disposable blade, available in most traditional types, including ryoba– and dozuki-nokogiri. A changeable blade's fine cutting edge stays sharp for a long time. These saws are especially good if you are learning to use a Japanese saw for the first time. If you put a kink into the blade or break some teeth, you can simply replace the blade, which costs only half as much as a new saw.

TOSHIO ODATE is a woodworker in Woodbury, Connecticut, and teaches sculpture and woodworking at New York's Pratt Institute. His book, *Japanese Woodworking Tools: Their Tradition, Spirit and Use,* is available from The Taunton Press.

Soup Up a Dovetail Saw

BY MARIO RODRIGUEZ

As a novice woodworker, I always marveled at those impossibly narrow-necked dovetails on 18th-century furniture. A chisel wouldn't have fit into such tiny openings, so it was obvious that the craftsmen didn't pare the joints. They must have cut them right the first time. I couldn't imagine cutting such tight kerfs and straight lines with any saw I owned.

A little later in my quest for perfect dovetails, I tried Japanese saws. They always cut beautifully and left a thin kerf, but I never warmed up to them. I worried about ruining their fragile but costly blades, and I couldn't get used to cutting on the pull stroke.

Now, years later, I use the same types of European-style dovetail saws I started with. But I don't use a saw before modifying the shape and set of its teeth, as the photos on this and the following pages show. The result is an American hybrid that cuts straight, whisper-thin kerfs.

The Trouble with New Dovetail Saws

When I buy a new saw, I find that it's usually in no shape to cut dovetails. The most common problems are too many teeth, too much set and an inappropriate tooth pattern.

Too many teeth One problem with dovetail saws is the number of teeth they have. Most dovetail saws have between 18 and 26 teeth per inch. Many woodworkers think that the more teeth a dovetail saw has, the smoother it will cut. That's not necessarily true. The more teeth a saw has, the more strokes it will take to reach the dovetail baseline. The more strokes it takes, the more

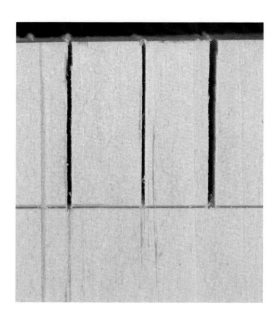

THINNEST AND STRAIGHTEST. The author's modified saw cut the center kerf. To the left is the kerf made by a Japanese saw, and to the right is the kerf of an off-the-shelf Western-style dovetail saw.

FOR BETTER CUTS, **refile teeth and reduce set.**

1 **Eliminate every other tooth.** Start at the heel of the blade between the first two teeth. Position the back edge of the file vertically, perpendicular to the blade. Begin the cut with about a quarter of the file's length past the blade. Push forward and slightly toward the toe, simultaneously filing away the front tooth and recutting the face of the rear tooth. Three strokes should take out the whole front tooth. Repeat until you reach the toe of the saw. The inset photo shows what the freshly cut teeth should look like.

the cut is likely to wander. On my modified saws, I've found that between 9 tpi and 12 tpi is about ideal.

Converting a saw with a lot of teeth is pretty straightforward: Just file away every other tooth. You may never have sharpened a saw, let alone altered the number of teeth, but it's actually a lot simpler than it sounds. A saw vise is helpful, but the blade can also be held in a regular woodworking vise or a machinist's vise, with wood strips on either side of the blade to grip and protect it. For both dovetail and tenon saws, I use a double, extra-slim taper saw file. These files are available at many hardware stores.

Too much set A bigger problem with a new saw is the set, the amount the teeth are bent away from the blade. Set allows the saw to cut a kerf wider than the blade is thick. This keeps the saw from binding or kinking. But most new saws have so much set that it's impossible to keep the saw cut-

2 Remove the set. Put the blade on an anvil or similar surface, and gently hammer out the set. Light taps will do the trick. Remember, you're just flattening a thin sawblade, not working horseshoes.

3 Set the teeth. For a dovetail saw used mostly on hardwoods, the author uses the minimum setting (the highest number) on the saw set. For a dovetail saw used mostly on softwoods or thin stock, he doesn't add any set.

4 Joint the teeth. Eliminating teeth and removing the set can create teeth of varying heights. Use a 10-in. mill file to take the tops of the teeth down until they are all at the same height.

ting to a precise line. For that reason, I start out by eliminating all the set on my dovetail saws. For a saw destined to cut dovetails in pine, I don't need any set. For a saw that I'll use on harder woods, I'll put back a little set. Tools that are used to make this adjustment (called saw sets) are available by mail and from antique-tool dealers.

Wrong tooth pattern The third problem is the tooth configuration. The teeth on dovetail saws are in a crosscut pattern: The teeth are angled back slightly for a better cut across the grain. But dovetails are cut

5 Sharpen the teeth. Keep the back edge of the file straight up and down, and file straight across the blade. Take light passes until you've brought each tooth to a sharp point, as in the inset photo. File all teeth from the same size.

6 Deburr the teeth. Filing the teeth will create burrs on the far side of the blade that can cause your saw to catch, drag, or wander slightly. To remove these burrs, just pass a coarse stone lightly across the blade.

7 Take the saw for a test drive. While using a slow, full stroke, notice whether the saw wanders (could be an uneven set) or wants to snag (possibly uneven tooth height). If you've prepared the saw carefully, it should cut true to a marked line, take few strokes to get to the baseline, and leave a thin kerf.

predominantly with the grain. So it made sense to me that a rip pattern, in which the leading edge of each tooth is perpendicular to the blade, might work better. When I eliminate the extra teeth, I file the leading edge of the remaining teeth straight up and down.

Practice First

If you're nervous about drastically altering the fancy, imported backsaw that cost $65, consider first overhauling a cheaper saw with a turned handle. Stanley makes a good one that retails for about $10. If you're happy with the results, then you can redo your pride and joy.

MARIO RODRIGUEZ is a contributing editor to *Fine Woodworking* magazine and the author of *Building Fireplace Mantels* (Taunton Press, 2002).

Sharpening Handsaws

BY FRED WILDER

Someone asked, "Will a sewing needle slide down the tooth edge of a carpenter's handsaw?" It was the end of another day on Attu Island, a barren, windswept speck of land at the end of the Aleutian chain. We were a bunch of homesick carpenter Seabees sitting around the stove in a Quonset hut, waiting for lights out. The question hung in the air, and then there was laughter. There wasn't much to do at night, but that last question really scraped the bottom of the barrel for a conversation topic.

Still, we were curious. One of the other carpenters retrieved a crosscut saw from his tool kit. We gathered around while he placed a needle on the teeth. When he tilted the saw, the needle ran down the edge like a streak of quicksilver. The question had been answered. But I knew it didn't mean that the saw was sharp, just that the blade was

HOW SHARP ARE YOUR SAWS?
You can learn a lot by looking down the tooth edge. Bends, kinks, and other defects readily show up.

straight and the teeth had been set and filed evenly.

Only the very points of the teeth do any cutting. They could be dull as ditch water and the needle would still slide just as fast because it doesn't ride on the points of the teeth, but between them. Even so, you could say that needle sliding does show something. If the needle slides well, you know that you're at least halfway to making a saw ready for the work it was designed to do.

TWO OR THREE GENTLE STROKES WITH THE JOINTER—You need only joint the teeth until the file touches the tops of the shortest teeth.

The Tools You'll Need for Sharpening

A jointer, a file, a saw clamp, a saw set, a hammer with a convex face, and an adjustable light are the main tools you'll need to sharpen your saw. You can make a perfectly good jointer by attaching an old 6-in. mill file to a block of wood. The file that I use to sharpen sawteeth is a 7-in. double extra-slim taper. It works fine for all teeth sizes. You can either buy an old saw clamp at a flea market or you can make one. You just need some way to put even clamping pressure along the blade.

A saw set bends the teeth so that they cut a kerf wider than the sawblade. My choice of saw sets is a Taintor. It has a thin washer that can be put under the set anvil to change the amount of tooth that is bent over. Saw sets with a fixed anvil height may set large teeth at the right height but will set small teeth too low. The Taintor also has a second plunger that clamps to the saw before the set plunger sets the tooth. This feature reduces the chances for error in holding the saw set on the tooth. I don't know of another saw set with both these features or one that is as comfortable to use. You'll have to keep an eye out for one at a flea market or yard sale, because they haven't been made for years.

Perhaps lighting isn't a tool, but it is important. Natural light is too unpredictable and is often hard to come by in a shop. Most of the time, I file using a shaded 100w bulb suspended on a cord, which allows for adjustment. I've found the best place for a light is in front of me, below the level of my eyes, and on the far side of the saw.

Straightening, Jointing, and Setting the Saw

I begin each sharpening by checking the blade for kinks and bends, even on the saws I use regularly (see the photo on p. 107).

After I get the blade perfectly straight, I joint and then set the saw. If the saw is just wood dull, it can be filed sharp a time or two without jointing or setting.

No matter how sharp, a saw will cut straight only if it's straight. Take out any bends by flexing the blade against the bend with your hands. Don't worry about over-bending the blade. I have bent saws quite severely to straighten them, and I've never had one break.

Unless a kink is severe and obvious, finding its exact location can be hard. Move the blade back and forth along its length in the light. Any kink will show up as a ripple in the reflection. Mark the whole kink with chalk, and then place the saw on a smooth hardwood board and hammer it flat. Any small hammer with a convex face, such as a ball peen, will do. Just don't use a hammer with a flat face because it will leave half-moon dents in your blade.

Before you set the teeth, make sure they are all the same height and the same shape. The jointer cuts the taller teeth even with the shorter ones. Run the jointer from the handle end to the point using light pressure (see the photo on the facing page). If a number of teeth remain untouched, make another pass with the jointer in the opposite direction, from point to handle. This will help keep the cut even.

If a saw has been run hard upon a nail or filed unevenly the last time it was sharpened, you will need to joint the teeth much more. In this case, you may end up with unevenly shaped teeth, some full size, some filed very flat. Before you set them, you will need to reshape these teeth (see the drawing in the sidebar at right).

Ideally, the tooth edge should have a slight crown from toe to heel of about ⅛ in. The crown lets the teeth cut progressively instead of all at once. This makes it easier to start a cut and easier to keep going.

Some saws are manufactured with a crowned tooth edge. To keep this crown, or

Reshaping Jointed Teeth before Setting

Some teeth may be much shorter than others after jointing. You must reshape them before setting. Pay attention to where the final point should be, and vary the pressure you put on the file accordingly—to the left, the right, or down.

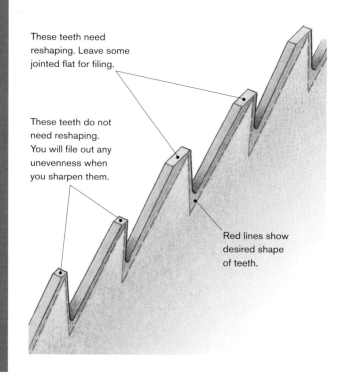

These teeth need reshaping. Leave some jointed flat for filing.

These teeth do not need reshaping. You will file out any unevenness when you sharpen them.

Red lines show desired shape of teeth.

make one, press down on the jointer harder near the ends of the blade or make another short pass at each end.

I prefer to sit down and hold the saw in my lap to set it (see the photo on p. 110). This way, the saw is at an angle, rather than my wrist. The advantage of this will be apparent if you try to set a 12 points-per-inch saw in a clamp: Your wrist won't be the same for a week. Use the teeth near the

IT'S EASIER TO MOVE THE SAW up your lap than to move the set down the saw (right). Only the top part of the tooth should be bent (top).

handle as a guide for how much set you should give the rest. As a general rule, bend the teeth out about half the thickness of the blade. If you cut mostly hard, dry wood, you'll need even less set. Watch the height of the anvil, and only set the top one-third to one-half of the tooth (see the left photo above). If it's set too low, the plunger can bend or dimple the saw plate and even break off teeth. Set a few teeth near the handle first and observe how well they match.

Proceed from handle to point, and then on the other side of the saw, from point to handle. Actually, I can't see that it makes much difference if you start at the point. Mark my advice down to habit. Set every other tooth, moving the saw set along with your left hand. Turn the saw around and set the other half of the teeth.

When you've finished, look at the set of the teeth by holding up the saw flat to the light. All the teeth should be uniform. If not, before you set them again, determine if the problem is the set or the way you're using it.

Filing the Teeth to Sharp Points

How you file the very tips of the teeth is more important than how you file the gullets and faces of the teeth. Only the very tips cut the wood. The gullets and faces just push the severed fibers out of the kerf. In filing, the key is to reduce the jointed flats to points all the same height.

How to hold the file Put the saw in the clamp, handle to your right, with the teeth about ⅜ in. above the clamp jaws. Adjust the light so that there is a good reflection from the jointed flats of the teeth, and be sure that you can see them clearly. Position yourself so that the file is an extension of your forearm. Hold the point of the file with your other hand. Filing this way will reduce strain on your wrist and elbow.

Put the file in a tooth gullet, holding it very lightly. Let the file float for a few inches, trying to find the angles before cutting. The angles you need to keep in mind depend on the kind of saw that you're sharpening: crosscut or rip (see the drawing on p.112). The bright area where the file has cut will tell you how good your angles are.

Reducing the flats to even points When you're comfortable that you're getting the right cutting angles, make several passes on the back side of the teeth that are set away from you. With just enough pressure to make the file cut, take only as many passes

as you need until the jointed flat at the top of the tooth is reduced by about one-half (see the photo below). Continue along the blade until all the teeth have been filed in this way. When I can't quite see a tooth, I have found that my thumbnail reflects light quite well when I put it behind the tooth.

Reverse the saw in the clamp. Position yourself with the file pointing toward the handle. Repeat the operation for the other half of the teeth, again reducing the amount of flat by about a half. When finished, return the sawblade to the original position. This time, file the points until a needle point of brightness remains. Reverse the saw and do the other teeth the same way.

The reason for two or more filings on a side is to keep the teeth all the same size. Although the file should cut mostly on the left of the gullet (the back side of the tooth), it also cuts some of the front side of the adjacent tooth (see the drawing on p. 112). If the filed teeth were brought up to sharpness on the first pass, filing the

AIM FOR ONLY HALF A SHINE AT FIRST. On the first pass, file the back of each tooth from the gullet up to the point, reducing the jointed flat by half. On the return pass, file the flats to sharp points. Remember that the only angle you change is the direction of the file.

Filing Angles

The drawings below show the three angles to consider when filing sawteeth. Angles don't need to be exact but should be as uniform as possible on each saw.

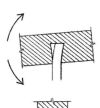

File's vertical angle affects only the ease of cut and the shape of the gullets. For all saws, hold file just under 90°.

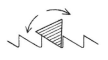

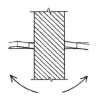

File's horizontal angle determines shape of the points of the teeth.

File's axial angle is determined by the tooth's hook. Hook is the angle between the front of the tooth and the cutting line of the saw. The greater the hook, the more aggressive the cut.

Crosscut Saw

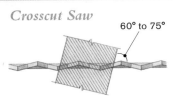

60° to 75°

Filing at this angle will make a pointed tooth appropriate for cutting across grain.

←————— Direction of cut

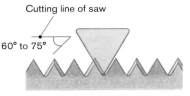

Cutting line of saw

60° to 75°

Crosscut teeth with little or no hook

←————— Direction of cut

Ripsaw

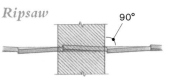

90°

Filing at this angle will make a chisel-shaped tooth appropriate for ripping.

←————— Direction of cut

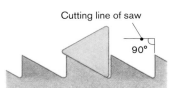

Cutting line of saw

90°

Ripsaw teeth with strong hook

←————— Direction of cut

return pass could excessively shorten some of the previously filed teeth.

Sometimes a thin bit of metal clings to the edge of the filed teeth. This is called a feather edge, and it reflects light, giving a false reading of the sharpness of the teeth. After you file the saw, make a cut with all the teeth to rub off the feather edge. Look at the teeth. Some will show a bit of jointed flat on the tip. File these teeth again.

Now find a sewing needle and answer the original question for yourself. Then

you'll know if you jointed and set the teeth evenly. But to see if it's sharp and will cut straight, there's no better test than that first cut.

FRED WILDER was a forester by education and has worked as a logger and carpenter. He ran workshops for the Civil Conservation Corps from 1939 to 1942 and served as a Seabee during World War II.

The Backsaw
Makes a Comeback

There is an old truth buried under mountains of machine-made sawdust—the best way to sever wood is with a thin, sharp blade. This is the beauty of the backsaw. With its swaged metal spine, a backsaw can carry the thinnest of blades, allowing it to slice wood with minimum waste and maximum control. No one can deny the aggressive speed of a tablesaw or a sliding chopsaw, but for joinery (and quiet pleasure) it's hard to beat the backsaw's surgical precision.

Another great thing about this most critical hand tool is that it is a whole lot cheaper than a screaming armada of cutting machines. A backsaw is one of the cheapest tools you can buy, especially if you plan to do lots of joinery by hand. Best of all, it doesn't take much to master. True, it involves some practice, but success with a backsaw is not so much about skill as it is about choosing the right saw and keeping it sharp.

Rips and Crosscuts Seldom Come in One Package

All wood saws do two things and two things only: they rip along the grain and crosscut across it. Follow the direction of the grain and you're ripping. Cut a board perpendicular to the grain and you're crosscutting. You might think a simple saw can do both with equal ease, and sometimes it can. But the ripsaw that seemed like a scalpel cutting dovetail pins might leave a crosscut, such as a tenon shoulder, looking a little chewed up.

BY ZACHARY GAULKIN

A Thin Blade Needs a Strong Back

The secret of the backsaw lies in its metal spine, which allows it to carry a thin blade. Whether you choose a European backsaw (left) or a Japanese dozuki (right), the backsaw is an essential hand tool for any woodworking shop.

PUSH VS. PULL TECHNOLOGY.
European saws cut on the push stroke, so they must be thick enough not to buckle or bend. Japanese saws can be thinner because they cut on the pull stroke, when the blade is in tension.

A BACKSAW HAS LIFE UNTIL THERE'S NO METAL LEFT. As long as the blade isn't bent or broken and rust hasn't invaded the steel, an old backsaw can be sharpened or retoothed to its original condition.

EUROPEAN RIP VS. CROSSCUT

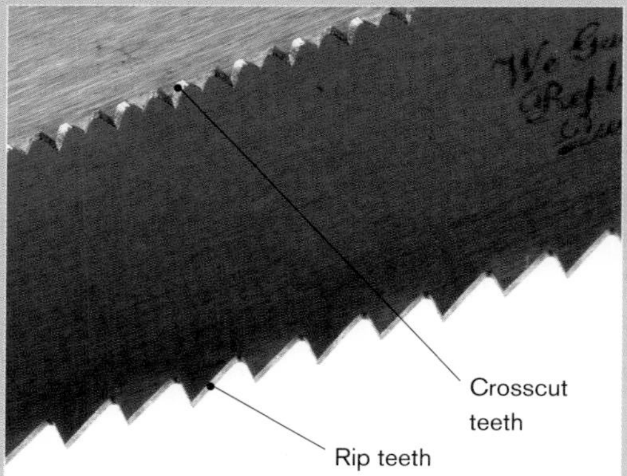

Crosscut teeth

Rip teeth

Rip teeth are usually larger than crosscut teeth, and they are filed straight across the steep leading edge. Crosscut teeth have bevels on the inside face to score and sever the grain.

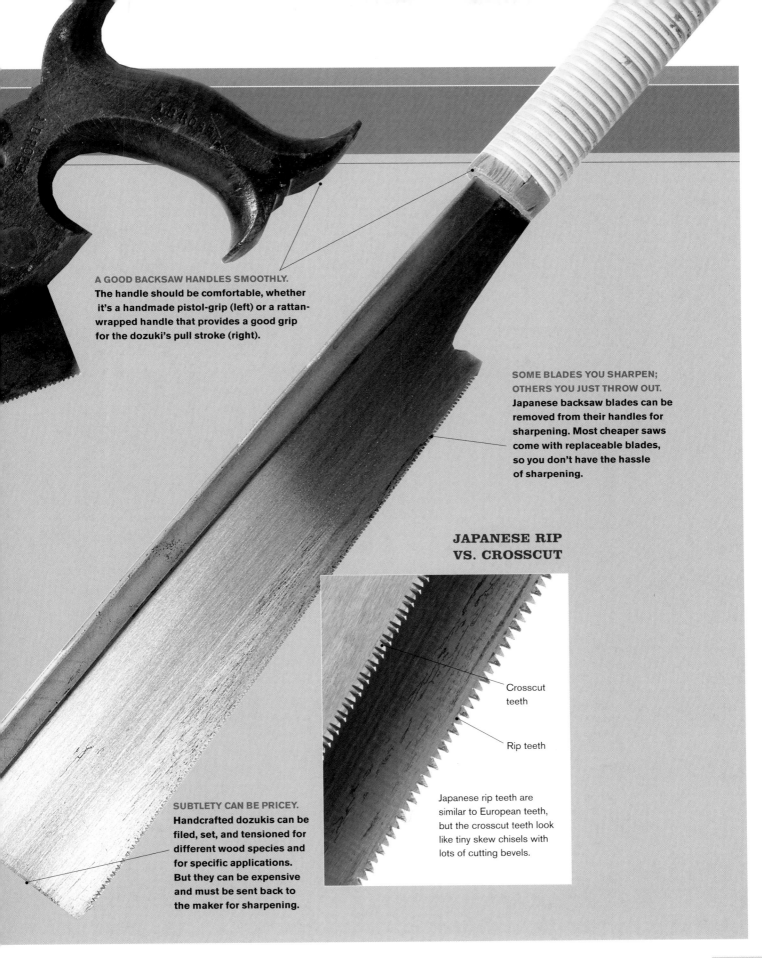

A GOOD BACKSAW HANDLES SMOOTHLY.
The handle should be comfortable, whether it's a handmade pistol-grip (left) or a rattan-wrapped handle that provides a good grip for the dozuki's pull stroke (right).

SOME BLADES YOU SHARPEN; OTHERS YOU JUST THROW OUT.
Japanese backsaw blades can be removed from their handles for sharpening. Most cheaper saws come with replaceable blades, so you don't have the hassle of sharpening.

JAPANESE RIP VS. CROSSCUT

Crosscut teeth

Rip teeth

Japanese rip teeth are similar to European teeth, but the crosscut teeth look like tiny skew chisels with lots of cutting bevels.

SUBTLETY CAN BE PRICEY.
Handcrafted dozukis can be filed, set, and tensioned for different wood species and for specific applications. But they can be expensive and must be sent back to the maker for sharpening.

Get a Grip

Backsaws come in many shapes and forms. Although the handles may differ, their defining characteristic is the metal back that supports and stiffens the thin blade. Unlike carpentry saws, backsaws have finer teeth and are used mainly for joinery.

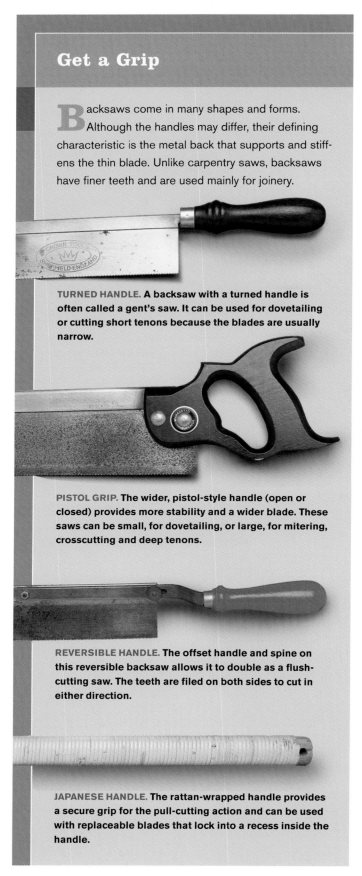

TURNED HANDLE. A backsaw with a turned handle is often called a gent's saw. It can be used for dovetailing or cutting short tenons because the blades are usually narrow.

PISTOL GRIP. The wider, pistol-style handle (open or closed) provides more stability and a wider blade. These saws can be small, for dovetailing, or large, for mitering, crosscutting and deep tenons.

REVERSIBLE HANDLE. The offset handle and spine on this reversible backsaw allows it to double as a flush-cutting saw. The teeth are filed on both sides to cut in either direction.

JAPANESE HANDLE. The rattan-wrapped handle provides a secure grip for the pull-cutting action and can be used with replaceable blades that lock into a recess inside the handle.

A saw's ability to rip or to crosscut lies in the geometry of its teeth—the size, shape, and set, or the amount they are bent away from the blade. Rip teeth usually are bigger than crosscut teeth, their cutting faces are nearly straight up and down and flat across, and they have a small amount of set. The big teeth shave away material fast, and the deep gullets (the valleys between the teeth) give the shavings a place to go so the saw won't bind. The small set on a rip tooth creates a narrow kerf, making it less likely to wander.

Crosscut teeth have more set, giving the body of the blade (sometimes called the plate) a wider path. The teeth are raked back (they don't have the steep leading edge of a rip tooth), and they are beveled to a point like an incisor, rather than filed straight across. These points enable a crosscut saw to score and sever the grain cleanly, without tearout.

Because backsaws are made for joinery and not for carpentry, the teeth tend to be small. The teeth still are filed for ripping or crosscutting, but the differences are not as noticeable as they are on big panel saws. So depending on your wallet and the level of perfection you hope to achieve, backsaws can be somewhat interchangeable. (In fact, most catalogs don't make a distinction between rip and crosscut backsaws; you have to ask.) It's certainly possible to rip with a crosscut backsaw (everybody does it), but it will take you longer, the teeth will probably get clogged with sawdust, and the kerf might be a little ragged. You can miter or cut a tenon shoulder with a backsaw ground for ripping, but you'll probably have to clean up a shaggy edge with a plane or a chisel.

The most common backsaws you will find are European or Western in style. They cut on the push stroke, and they come in many styles: rip and crosscut, pistol grips and turned handles, long and short, brass-backed, and even reversible (see the photos on the facing page). They can have more or less set, and the teeth can be big, aggressive ones or small, fine ones. More teeth per inch generally mean that you will get a finer, slower cut. (Backsaws range from 12 tpi to more than 20 tpi.)

Wil Neptune, an instructor at the North Bennet Street School in Boston, suggests that if you only want one European-style backsaw it makes sense to get one that can rip well. That's because most joinery cuts—tenon cheeks and dovetails—are made along the grain, not across it. With a steady hand and sharp teeth, you can slice your dovetails without having to clean up the ripcuts with a chisel. (You'll still have to chisel the shoulder, of course.) For cross-cuts, such as tenon shoulders, you can get away with using the same saw by cutting to the waste side of the line and cleaning up the edge with a chisel. As Neptune points out, you rarely try to get a finished crosscut surface off the saw anyway.

Japanese Saws Give New Meaning to Severance Pay

The variety of European backsaws is nothing compared with the Japanese equivalent, called a dozuki. What's the difference? There are many, but chief among them is that Japanese saws cut on the pull stroke, when the blade is in tension and won't buckle or bend. This means a Japanese saw

It's No Crime to Leave the Sharpening to a Professional

Using a backsaw is a pleasure. Sharpening one is another story. Some people try, but few can do it well. Most woodworkers don't even think about it until the thing just refuses to cut anymore. Sharpening your own saws is a valuable skill, but for most of us, it makes more sense to seek out professional help. A good sharpening service, though sometimes hard to find, can turn a rusty antique into a precision instrument or customize a new saw right out of the package.

If you're not sure whether your saw needs sharpening, it probably does. Even new saws need to be touched up. New backsaws generally come with punched teeth (one side of the saw is rolled over, and the other side has a slight burr) and therefore cut more aggressively on one side. Filing, either by hand or machine, cleans up the edges and solves the problem.

A professional sharpener can also reduce or increase the set, depending on what kind of use you have in mind. (Many woodworkers say new backsaws come with far too much set.)

Sharpeners can file the teeth on old backsaws, or they can do much more, as long as the steel is solid and the blade isn't bent or warped. They can change the angle and set of the teeth or even retooth the saw entirely.

SHARPENING A BACKSAW IS A SKILL. A single pass will sharpen the teeth on this dovetail saw. Each stroke has to be even to keep the teeth uniform.

My Favorite Backsaw: If You Could Have Just One, Which Would It Be?

Wil Neptune's Orange-Handled Beauty Is a Bargain

What saw does cabinetmaker and teacher Wil Neptune reach for to cut a dovetail or tenon by hand? "That's easy," he says. "It's the cheesy one with the blue blade and the painted orange handle." It costs $9.95* and has become a staple in the student toolboxes at the North Bennet Street School in Boston, where Neptune teaches woodworking. The saw comes from the factory a little rough. So he shows his students how to file the teeth and press out some of the set by sandwiching the blade between two old jointer knives and clamping it in a machinist's vise. "If you totally screw it up, throw it in a drywall bucket for site work, and buy a new one." The Eberle saw and file is available from J. I. Joseph Co. (617-723-2323).

A Handmade Dozuki Can Track a Line Like a Bloodhound

John Reed Fox, a furniture maker in Acton, Mass., has a simple philosophy about tools. If you are at all serious, buy the best you can afford. That's one of the reasons his favorite backsaw is a handmade dozuki crafted to his specifications. His dozukis, which he sends back to Japan every year or so for sharpening, are a dream to use. With a little camellia oil (a traditional Japanese saw lubricant), it can follow a line like a bloodhound tracking a scent. Fox recently let a class of novice woodworking students use one of his dozukis to cut dovetails. "People were nailing the cuts right on the line, and they were rank beginners," he says. "Everybody was astonished." A similar handmade saw is available for about $100 from Misugi Design (510-549-0805).

The Antique Miter Saw Revived for Ripping

Allan Breed doesn't even know where his favorite backsaw came from. It's an old Henry Taylor, one of about a dozen backsaws he owns. After Breed reground the teeth for ripping, it has become his favorite dovetail saw, perfect for his unusual tail-cutting technique: With the workpiece flat on a bench, he dangles the saw from his pinkie with the teeth pointing away from his body. This plumbs the saw, guaranteeing a square cut across the end grain. He plunges through each cut in two or three swipes (still hanging on by his pinkie finger) and moves onto the next one. "I can see what I'm doing, and it's more comfortable," he says. "I also wax my saws a lot, especially if there isn't a ton of set in them. It makes it a lot easier." For a good used saw, look around at yard sales and used-tool suppliers.

can carry a thinner blade than its European counterpart (although the difference, again, is less apparent on backsaws than on saws made for carpentry).

There is also a dental difference: Rip teeth on a Japanese saw closely resemble Western rip teeth. The cutting edge is nearly perpendicular to the blade, and the teeth come to points. But Japanese crosscut teeth are quite different from their Western counterparts. They have an angled top (the profile sort of resembles a skew chisel), and each facet is beveled. "They've got bevels all over the place," says John Reed Fox, a cabinetmaker in Acton, Mass., who uses Japanese handsaws almost exclusively.

You can go crazy choosing a dozuki, especially if you have an unlimited budget. A good Japanese saw smith can take into account things like wood density and moisture content, and can even tailor a saw to match the idiosyncrasies of a single woodworker's stroke. Subtlety comes at a price, though. Fox spends more than $100 for his handmade dozukis, which he sends back to Japan for sharpening. If you can't justify investing in a handmade saw, you can buy factory-made Japanese backsaws with replaceable blades for $50 or less. When the blade gets dull or breaks, just buy a new one. According to those who swear by them, even cheap dozukis outperform good European-style saws.

A Saw's True Worth Is Measured in Decibels

When is a whispering backsaw better than a power saw? It depends on whom you ask. Wil Neptune can cut a perfect tenon with a backsaw and chisel in minutes, leaving a thimbleful of sawdust. But he does so only on occasion. Machines are just too efficient if you have to make more than one, he says, "and when do you ever make something

with one tenon?" But if he needs to miter something quickly or if an unusual joint requires lots of set-up time on a machine, a backsaw can be quite handy.

Dovetails are another story. Allan Breed, a Maine cabinetmaker, does all his dovetails by hand, racing through the cuts with an old miter saw reground for ripping. "I'll cut dovetails with anything as long as it's sharp," he says. Breed doesn't use handsaws for some romantic thrill. He does it for ergonomics and efficiency. Power saws and routers are loud, and you have to haul around a lot of metal. And on the kind of high-style reproductions that Breed makes, tooling up with machines hardly ever makes sense. For Fox, handsaws are a critical part of the work itself. With a handsaw, he can cut perfect dovetails less than an eighth of an inch apart, something no machine has yet been able to accomplish.

* Please note price estimates are from 1998.

ZACHARY GAULKIN is a former editor of *Fine Woodworking* magazine.

Build a Bowsaw

BY J. CRATE LARKIN

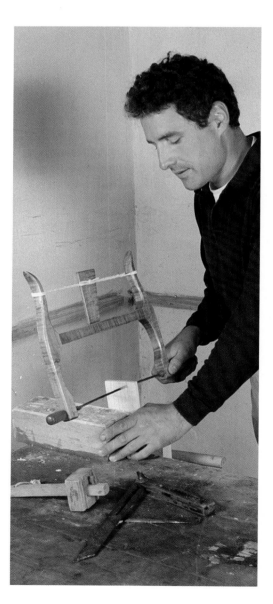

As a full-time woodworker, I have a lot of power-tool options in my shop. But there are occasions when it's simply faster and easier to use a hand tool to get the job done. And one I reach for all the time is the bowsaw, a tool that's been serving woodworkers for centuries. At first glance the saw might seem charmingly primitive. Yet the engineering is remarkably ingenious.

Over the years bowsaws have been made in various sizes. This one is an adaptation of several 18th-century English and Continental designs. With a 12-in.-long blade, it's both compact and light, so it gets used in all sorts of ways. For example, it's the tool I reach for when I need to crosscut a few parts quickly to rough length. I also use it like a scroll saw to cut curved shapes. The bowsaw also lends itself to cutting angles. And with the blade turned 90 degrees, I sometimes even rip a board with the saw. You can get the steel blade from a couple of mail-order outfits (see Sources on p. 124). The blade is available with either 8, 9, 12, or 16 teeth per inch. For most cuts, the 8-tpi or 9-tpi blade works just fine.

Tensioning the blade is easy. A thin, tapered piece of wood—called a key— twists a length of leather cord, which pulls together the top ends of the saw's two long

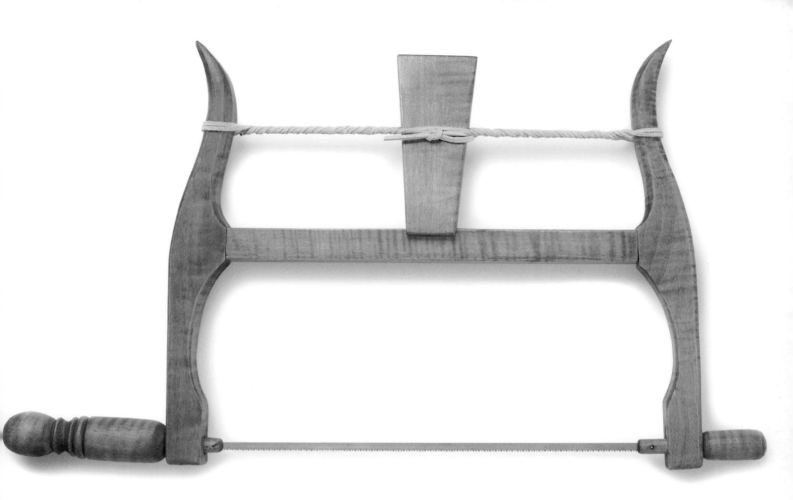

arms, called brackets. That action forces apart the bottom ends of the brackets, putting the blade under tension.

Start by Making the Wood Parts

The bowsaw is made up of just six wood parts: the two brackets and the key, plus a stretcher, handle, and knob. You'll need about 2 bd. ft. of ⅞-in.-thick stock and an 8-in.-long piece of 1¼-in. square stock.

When the saw is assembled and tensioned, all of the parts end up under some stress, so it makes sense to use hardwood stock. Maple, birch, or beech are good choices, but to make the saw look as nice as it works, I went one step further and used curly maple.

The brackets are first Begin by cutting out two pieces of stock for the brackets. They'll be cut to final shape on the bandsaw, so make them a little wider and longer than necessary.

Now transfer the bracket pattern (see the drawing on p. 122) to a piece of heavy paper or cardboard. Cut the pattern to shape with scissors, then place it on the bracket stock and trace the profile with a pencil.

It takes just a few minutes to cut out the brackets on the bandsaw. Make the cut just outside the scribed line, then sand the parts to the line.

Give all sharp edges a good rounding over with a spokeshave, then follow with a file. Finish up by sanding each bracket up to 220 grit.

With the rounding and sanding completed, lay out the location of the single mortise in each bracket. Once the mortise locations have been marked, use a drill bit to remove most of the waste. A little work with a mortising chisel cleans up what remains.

At this point, the work on the brackets is just about completed. You just need to

Brackets Add Strength and Style

SCRIBE THE CURVED PROFILE ON THE BRACKETS. Using a paper pattern of the bracket profile, transfer the curved shape to ⅞-in.-thick stock.

A SPOKESHAVE SOFTENS THE EDGES. The bracket is kinder on the hands if the edges are well-rounded.

EACH BRACKET HAS A SINGLE MORTISE. Cutting the mortise is a two-step process. First drill a couple of holes to remove most of the waste material, then use a sharp mortising chisel to clean up what remains.

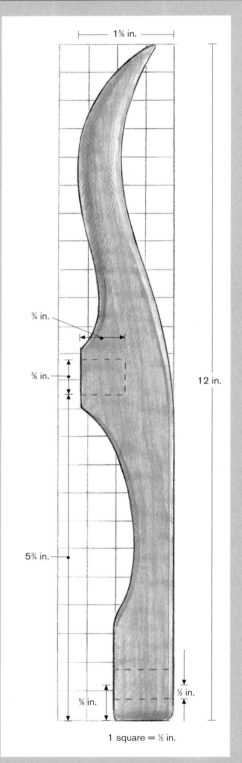

1⅝ in.

12 in.

¾ in.

⅝ in.

5¾ in.

⅝ in.

½ in.

1 square = ½ in.

THE PARTS OF A BOWSAW

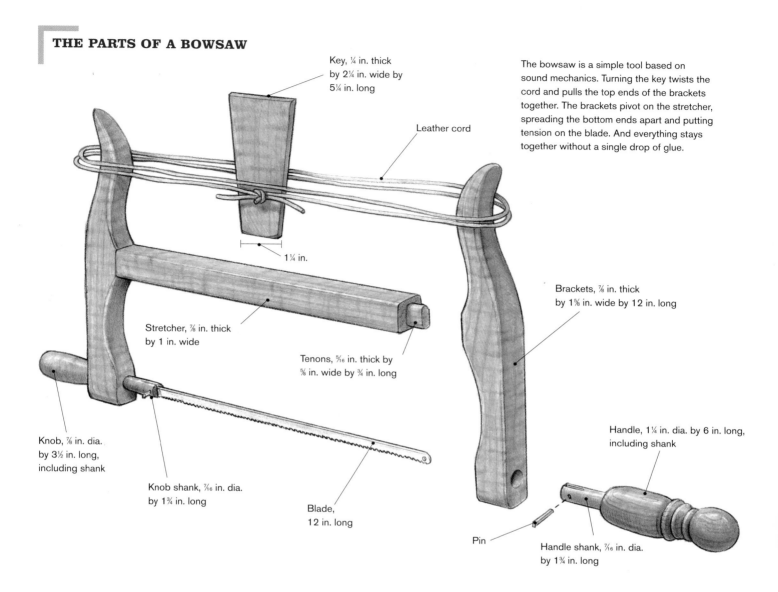

Key, ¼ in. thick by 2¼ in. wide by 5¼ in. long

Leather cord

The bowsaw is a simple tool based on sound mechanics. Turning the key twists the cord and pulls the top ends of the brackets together. The brackets pivot on the stretcher, spreading the bottom ends apart and putting tension on the blade. And everything stays together without a single drop of glue.

1¼ in.

Brackets, ⅞ in. thick by 1⅝ in. wide by 12 in. long

Stretcher, ⅞ in. thick by 1 in. wide

Tenons, ⁵⁄₁₆ in. thick by ⅝ in. wide by ¾ in. long

Knob, ⅞ in. dia. by 3½ in. long, including shank

Knob shank, ⁷⁄₁₆ in. dia. by 1¾ in. long

Blade, 12 in. long

Handle, 1¼ in. dia. by 6 in. long, including shank

Pin

Handle shank, ⁷⁄₁₆ in. dia. by 1¾ in. long

bore a ½-in.-dia. through-hole near the bottom of each one. Later, when the bowsaw is assembled, the shanks of the handle and knob are going to slip into these holes.

The stretcher connects the two brackets

The stretcher is simply a narrow length of stock with a tenon on each end that fits into a mortise in each bracket. I cut the tenons by establishing both the cheeks and shoulders on my bandsaw. The distance between the shoulders of the stretchers should be such that, when the stretcher is assembled, the ends of the blade will just meet the inside face of the lower end of the bracket.

One point to keep in mind here: Because the brackets must be free to pivot on the shoulders of the stretchers, the stretcher tenons are not glued into the bracket mortises. To allow the bracket to pivot just slightly, you need to make the tenons a little undersized.

The handle and knob anchor the blade

It takes only a few minutes to turn the handle and knob on the lathe. Make the shanks extralong, and keep a close eye on their diameters. You want them to slip smoothly into the holes that you drilled in the brackets.

Remove the handle and knob from the lathe, then trim the shanks to final length. Simply slip the shanks into the bracket holes and mark the cutoff point. I generally like to have at least ¾ in. extending through the bracket.

Once the shanks have been trimmed, use the bandsaw to cut a kerf in each one so that they will accept the ends of the blade. Then test-fit the blade in the kerfs. If the fit is too tight, you'll have to do some sanding to open the kerfs a little.

The blade is held in place by two pins that slip through each shank and then through the corresponding factory-drilled holes in the blade. For pins I prefer to use old-fashioned ½-in.-long cut nails, but 4d finish nails are an adequate substitute. By the way, it's not a bad idea to file down the pointed ends of the pins. Sharp points always seem to attract soft skin.

Position the ends of the blade next to the shanks and mark the hole locations on the shanks with a pencil. Then drill holes just big enough to accept the pins. Be sure to drill the holes at right angles to the kerfs in the shanks. After that, line up the holes in the shanks and blade and tap the pins through. There is no reason to worry about the pins falling out when you're using the saw. When the blade is under tension, the pins stay put.

The key Is a crank It's just a thin, tapered piece of wood, but the key is an important part of the bowsaw. It works like a simple crank, providing the leverage needed to twist the leather cord and apply tension to the blade. And after the blade has been tensioned, the narrow end of the key slips behind the stretcher, preventing the cord from unraveling.

Once the stock for the key has been cut to size, use a bevel gauge to scribe the two tapers along the edges. Then cut the tapers and plane the edges smooth. I also like to round all of the edges. That way, when I'm cranking the key, it feels a little more comfortable in my hand.

Apply the Finish

After the key has been made, it's time to apply a finish to all of the wood parts. First, though, do some final smoothing with 0000 steel wool.

To make the figured grain really stand out, I applied a single coat of aniline dye (early American maple).

When the dye dries, I like to apply at least three coats of Minwax® Antique Oil Finish. It builds to a smooth, lustrous finish that looks great on a tool like this.

Assemble the Saw

Slip the handle and knob into the holes in the brackets, then add the blade and pins. If you prefer to cut on the push stroke, the teeth of the blade should face away from the handle. If you like to cut on the pull stroke, as I do, face the teeth toward the handle. Once the blade has been installed, insert the stretcher tenons into the mortises in the brackets. Remember, though, there's no glue used here.

Now add the cord. I've used rawhide shoelaces in the past, but they don't hold up well. I've had better luck buying ¼-in. leather cord from a local fabric retailer.

Wrap the cord twice around the tops of the brackets. Pull the cord slightly taut, and tie the ends in a square knot. Next, slip the key between the rawhide, and turn (the direction it's turned doesn't matter) until the tension on the blade is enough to prevent it from bowing when making a cut. Slide the narrow end of the key behind the stretcher to keep the cord from unwinding, and you're ready to work.

J. CRATE LARKIN builds furniture and handtools in Woodsboro, Maryland.

Make the Handle

SHAPE IT ON THE LATHE. Once a blank for the handle has been mounted in the lathe, it takes just a few minutes to turn a profile that's both interesting and comfortable.

THE SHANK GETS A NARROW SLOT. Feeding the end of the shank into the bandsaw creates a near-perfect kerf for the bow-saw blade.

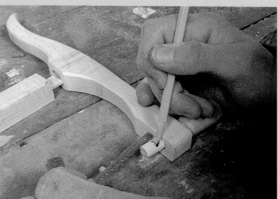

MARK THE HOLES FOR THE BLADE PINS. Use the blade to determine the exact locations of the holes on the shanks.

Simple Tools Can Reproduce Most Moldings

BY ROBERT S. JUDD

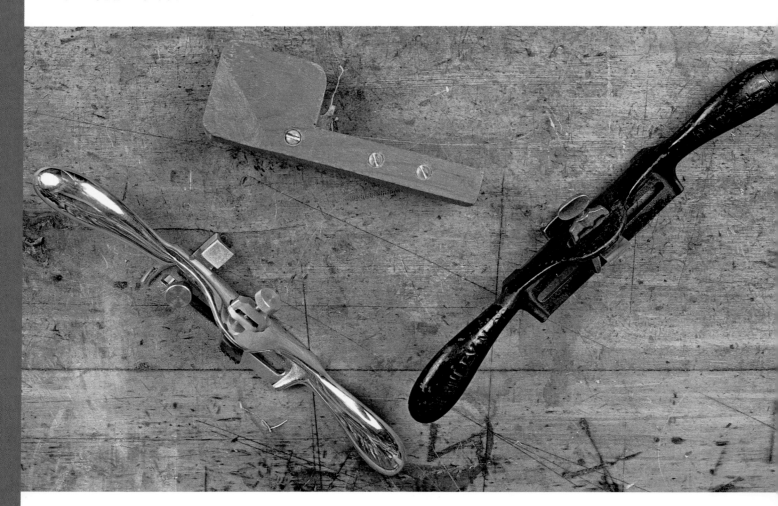

SCRATCH STOCKS. Whether old like the Stanley No. 66 (right), new like the Lie-Nielsen No. 66 reproduction (left), or shop-made (top), these scratch stocks are a simple way to reproduce moldings or create new designs accurately and economically.

Scratch stocks function beautifully, quickly, and economically to duplicate handworked wood trim. By simply grinding or filing a cutter to the appropriate profile, you can reproduce almost any shape molding up to about 1 in. wide. Scratch stocks, or beading tools as they are sometimes called, are readily available new (see sources), used (antique-tool dealers, garage sales, or flea markets) or shopmade (see the photo on the facing page). I make mine from a 6-in.-long, L-shaped piece of stock. The cutter fits into a sawkerf, and it is clamped in place with a few screws. The cutters for all of these tools are easily shaped from old scrapers and sawblades or new blanks from Lie-Nielsen or Lee Valley Tools.

In my repair and restoration business, I often need to duplicate broken or missing moldings. Usually, only a foot or two of the molding is needed: hardly worth the effort of setting up the router and definitely not worth having a cutter ground to match one of the myriad of molding shapes. Besides, no power tool can match the irregularities of the handworked wood found in older pieces.

Scratch Stocks and Beaders

First made by users as a simple holder for a scraper blade, scratch stocks included a fence arrangement to work a measured distance from an edge. The beading tool was essentially an improved, factory-made scratch stock and included a range of cutters in different sizes and several blanks, custom-filed to fit the user's needs. Adjustable fences for both straight and curved edges were often included. A scratch stock or beader can produce a carbon copy of the original molding by using a cutter that's simply filed to shape.

Shaping the Cutter

To make a basic beaded molding, take a sample piece of beading, a file, and a blade

FILING A CUTTER TO SHAPE. Almost any profile, up to 1 in. wide, can be filed into blade blanks made from old cabinet scrapers, sawblades or new blank stock.

blank and set to work filing a negative pattern of the molding, as shown in the photo above. As you file the pattern into the blade, keep testing its fit. Check the fit frequently because it is fairly easy to file past the desired shape. It's a good idea to leave a ⅛-in.-wide metal strip at either edge of the cutter. Narrower strips tend to bend and lose their effectiveness. Old cabinet scrapers or sawblade sections make good cutters for shopmade scratch stocks. But for my 100-year-old Stanley No. 66 hand beader, the blanks that Lie-Nielsen makes for his gemlike bronze replicas of the No. 66 work well. The steel of the new blanks is not hardened, so the blanks are easy to file to shape. After filing them to shape, hone just the cutter's faces on a whetstone to provide a clean cutting edge. I've never found it necessary to harden a cutter once it's filed to shape.

Making Moldings

When producing short moldings, I've found it easier to work the edge of my board, as shown in the left photo on p. 128. For making small beads or moldings, I cut two lengths at once by working both corners of the same board edge. Begin the

BEADING IS SIMPLE WITH A SCRATCH STOCK. Just hold the fence against the stock and make repeated passes, about ⅟₁₆ in. per pass, until the appropriate depth has been reached.

MATCHING A MOLDING TO A CUTTER is crucial to reproducing old moldings. File the cutter to the negative image of the molding. Check the cutter frequently while filing to make sure it is an accurate match.

scraping process by firmly gripping the handles, and push or pull the tool across the board's edge, keeping the handles at 90 degrees to the work. Take small scrapings initially, only ⅟₁₆ in. or so at a time. Because stock removal is done by scraping, a small cut gives much more control and does less damage if you slip. As the cutter starts to bottom out, you can continuously adjust the blade so more is exposed. In a surprisingly short time, the molding will start to appear on the edge. If the cutter starts to chatter or jump, you are probably trying to remove too much material, or the grain might be changing; use a little less pressure, or try changing the direction of cut.

One of the handy features of the No. 66 or the Lie-Nielsen reproduction is the adjustable fence. When cutting two lengths of molding on a board edge, the fence can be set to cut the opposite corner without moving the blade. This lets you produce a surprising amount of molding in a relatively short time. I make several extra moldings, so I can pick the best match to the original.

I like to start the staining and coloring process at this stage because the strips are far easier to handle while they are still attached to a board. Often, I will even do the preliminary finishing and filling at this point for the same reason. It's then a simple matter to trim the finished molding off on the tablesaw. I set the saw fence to leave a little extra material, which I later trim off with a utility knife.

When repairing antique pieces, mark your name and date on the back of the new molding for historical reference. After all, with a matching stain and finish, the repair should be almost invisible.

Other Applications

In addition to producing molding patterns, this highly functional family of tools is also effective for routing and inlay work. Because you create the cutters to fit the situation at hand, you are no longer limited to standard router bits.

When using these tools to rout cross-grain, however, it's a good idea to lay out the material to be removed by lightly cutting in the lines with a sharp craft knife. The scored lines help prevent tearout, which could ruin your project.

ROBERT S. JUDD is a professional furniture repairer and refinisher in Canton, Massachusetts.

Files, Rasps, and Rifflers

BY MARIO RODRIGUEZ

Rasps and files have all but disappeared from most woodworkers' toolboxes. Why? Well, there are a number of reasons. Routers and drum sanders do a lot of the shaping that rasps and files used to do. Because it's easy to damage files and rasps, many woodworkers consider them more of a pain than they're worth. And it can be hard to figure out what kind of file or rasp you need. What, for instance, is the difference between a second-cut patternmaker's rasp and a bastard-cut mill file?

But much is to be gained by adding rasps and files to your tool kit: greater speed and control in shaping curved or sculptural elements and dramatically reduced sanding time. By using a succession of rasps and files, I can start sanding at 180- or 220-grit. And because individual teeth are doing the cutting rather than a single blade, there's no danger of tearout. Rasps and files are the fastest, most efficient tools for removing lots of material quickly, for fairing curves, and for shaping furniture parts. Using rasps and files may be new to many woodworkers, but once you've started, you sure won't miss all that sanding.

The care and cleaning of these tools isn't complicated, as the sidebar on p. 132 explains. And a basic kit of the most useful

RASPS AND FILES ARE THE AUTHOR'S CHOICE for shaping wood. There's no tearout on figured woods, and a file can produce a surface very nearly ready to finish.

files and rasps doesn't have to be expensive and can be assembled gradually (see the sidebar on the facing page).

What Are Rasps Used For?

Rasps actually can be considered a type of file, but unlike files, rasps have individual conelike teeth, which are made by a punch striking the soft steel blank (see the middle photo below). These teeth are large and pointed, with deep gullets that keep the rasp from clogging. Each tooth and its gul-

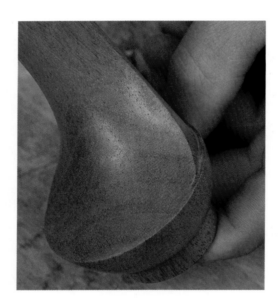

FILED, NOT SANDED. The author put a coat of shellac on this cabriole leg after shaping it with a file, but without sanding it. Only minor tool marks are still visible.

RASP TEETH (ABOVE) ARE FORMED INDIVIDUALLY when the steel blank is struck by a punch. The tooth and gullet are formed simultaneously. The two best rasps sold today are the Nicholson #49 and #50. The #49 removes a lot of wood quickly. The #50 leaves a smoother surface.

let are formed with a single blow from the punch. This process is called stitching.

On some imported rasps the teeth are hand-stitched, resulting in a slightly random pattern. Some woodworkers claim that these rasps produce a smoother cut with less chatter, but the hand-stitched rasps that I've used were no better than standard rasps that cost substantially less.

A rasp is the best tool for any sculptural shaping. It's designed to remove bandsaw-blade marks or the facets left by a spoke-shave, and it's used to produce smooth, fair curves. You should always use the longest rasp that your task will permit. In the same way that a plane with a long sole is used to level and flatten a board, a longer rasp does a better job of smoothing dips or bumps in curved work than a shorter one will.

Rasps are classified by shape, group, and cut Woodworker's rasps range in length from 6 in. to 14 in. and are flat, half round, or round in section, tapering slightly along their length. Half-round rasps are the most common. Rasps may have square, ta-pered, or pointed ends.

Woodworking rasps fall into three main groups (listed in descending order of coarseness): wood rasps, cabinet rasps, and patternmaker's rasps. Within these groups, rasps are further categorized, in descending order of coarseness, as bastard cut, second cut, and smooth cut. In the United States, the best rasps are made by Nicholson® (see Sources). Nicholson's #49 and #50 rasps (the #49 is a second-cut patternmaker's rasp and the #50 is a smooth-cut rasp) do all the rough-shaping work I expect from a rasp (see the bottom photo at left). For a list of recommended rasps and files, see the sidebar on the facing page.

Also, keep in mind that a shorter rasp will produce a finer finish than a longer rasp of the same cut. That's because the tooth spacing on rasps is proportional to the tool's length, closer together on shorter rasps, farther apart on longer rasps. An 8-in. second-cut rasp will leave a smoother surface than a 10-in. second-cut rasp. This rule of thumb is true for files as well.

Using a rasp It takes practice to learn how to use a rasp properly. First, put a handle on your new rasp. I don't believe that tale about someone jamming the tang through his palm, but a handle does make a rasp easier and more comfortable to use. A handle also provides the necessary length and grip for you to develop a smooth, rhythmic stroke.

The way to hold a rasp or file is with one hand on the handle and the other on the tip of the rasp between thumb and forefinger (see the photo below). If holding the tip is uncomfortable for you, wrap masking tape around it to provide a cushion.

Angle the rasp about 30 degrees to the workpiece and push forward, applying light pressure. Lift the rasp off the workpiece on the return stroke. Remember, you're shaping wood, not grating cheese. If you want to remove stock more aggressively, apply more pressure. If you want a finer surface, lighten up or switch to a finer rasp or a file. This stroke will produce the best results in the shortest time with the least wear and tear on the tool.

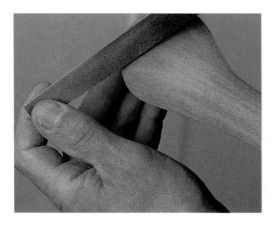

FOR BEST CONTROL, USE TWO HANDS. Grasp the file or rasp handle with one hand and hold the steel tip between thumb and forefinger of the other hand.

A Basic Selection of Files and Rasps

Here are a few of the rasps and files that I use most in my shop. I selected them for their usefulness, versatility, durability, and value. Naturally, you can get started with less and add to your kit later. With a few notable exceptions, most of these files can be purchased for $5* to $10. The exceptions are Nicholson rasps, which typically run $30 to $40 each; the Grobet detailing file (about $25); and a good set of rifflers, which can cost $100 or more. Avoid the cheap riffler sets because they wear quickly and perform poorly right from the start.

1) #49 Nicholson patternmaker's rasp: For heavy cutting and rough shaping of sculptural furniture elements, such as cabriole legs or broadly curved pieces, such as table aprons.

2) #50 Nicholson patternmaker's rasp: For a finer cut and smoother surface after using the #49. The smoother surface left by the #50 will more readily reveal dips, bumps, and other minor imperfections.

3) 8-in. bastard-cut round file: I use this file for shaping and fairing tight inside curves and for shaping replacement molding-plane blades.

4) l0-in. bastard-cut mill file: Will leave a very fine surface on wood, but I use it primarily for truing cabinet scrapers.

5) 6-in. second-cut mill file: Good general-purpose shop file. Excellent for cleaning up exposed end grain. I also use it frequently for deburring metal edges on machines, hand tools, or jig and fixture materials.

6) l0-in. second-cut, half-round file: Used for cleaning up after the #50 rasp.

7) 8-in. second-cut, half-round file: I use this for smoothing the surface left by the l0-in. half-round file. Because it's shorter, it leaves a finer surface, even though it's the same grade.

8) Grobet detail file: All-purpose detail file. This is probably the most-used file in my kit. I use it for all sorts of detail work.

9) Set of file rifflers (one end coarse, the other fine): For detailed shaping of carved ornaments, such as ball-and-claw feet, for sculptural drawer pulls, and for tool handles.

Care and Cleaning of Rasps and Files

Rasps and files are heat-treated to make them about as hard as a woodworking chisel (Rockwell hardness rating of Rc60 to Rc68). This makes them effective cutting tools on wood, aluminum, brass, and other nonferrous metals. And some files even can be used on soft (or annealed) steel. But because they've been hardened, files and rasps must be kept apart to prevent them from rubbing or banging together. Careless treatment might chip or dull the teeth and shorten file life. I store mine on a wall-mounted rack, like chisels. The blades are kept apart, and I can spot the one I need at a glance. I've also seen them stored in drawers, where slots or dividers keep the tools separated.

With use, files and rasps will clog. They can be cleaned with a file card. This is a small, flat, wooden paddle with stiff wire needles on one side and short plastic bristles on the other. Occasionally, when stubborn debris becomes lodged in the teeth, I'll run a wire finishing nail along the teeth. The nail's tip quickly will wear down to conform to the file's teeth and will dislodge any clogged material without damaging the file.

Files don't last forever. When a file starts to slide over your work-piece instead of cutting, it's best to get rid of it and buy a new one. A dull file will only become a source of frustration as well as a big waste of your time. A sharp file cuts easily and leaves a smooth surface in its wake.

FILE CARD CLEANS RASPS AND FILES. Clean rasps and files cut more effectively. File cards generally have a brush side and a wire side.

Files

Although rasps cut quickly, even the finest will leave a rough surface. The next step in shaping is filing, which can leave a surface that's nearly ready for finishing (see the top photo on p. 130).

Files are classified by size, shape and cut Files range in length from 4 in. to 16 in. and come in a variety of shapes and cross sections, each designed to perform a different task. There are square, flat, half-round, triangular, and round files. Half-round files, which are rounded on one side and flat on the other, are probably the most useful to woodworkers. Both sides have teeth, so you can use the flat side for convex and flat surfaces and the half-round side for concave work. Flat files also are useful for shaping long sections with curved profiles, such as cabriole legs. Round files are handy for shaping tight, inside curves.

All files are either single cut or double cut. Single-cut files have a single set of parallel teeth extending the length of the file. Double-cut files have two sets of intersecting teeth, creating diamond-shaped teeth, which leave smoother finishes than single-cut files. A single-cut file with a rectangular profile is called a mill file. A double-cut file with the same profile is called a flat file.

There are three grades of coarseness for files, and they are the same as for rasps: bastard cut, second cut, and smooth cut. And like a rasp, a file's length affects the coarseness of cut. Theoretically, each of these grades is available both single cut and double cut, but the double cut is more common. Most of the files I use are double cut.

One file that I use all the time doesn't fit neatly into any category. It's called a detailing file and is made by Grobet, a Swiss company. It's a double-ended (no tang) half-round file with a bastard cut at one end and a second cut on the other (see the top right photo on p. 133). This file costs

TOOTH SPACING IS PROPORTIONAL TO SIZE. **Both of these files are bastard cuts, but the teeth on the thinner, 8-in. file on the left are closer than on the 10-in. file on the right.**

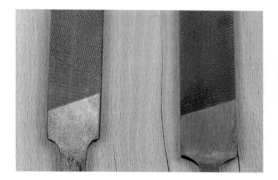

DOUBLE-CUT (LEFT) AND SINGLE-CUT FILES. **All grades of files are available as single or double cut. Double-cut files require more pressure, but they'll cut faster than single-cut files.**

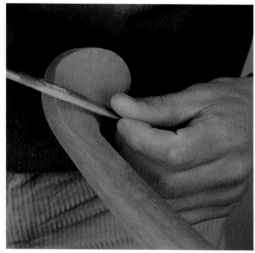

GROBET DETAILING FILE IS IN-DISPENSABLE. **Its half-round profile provides a flat side for flat and convex work and a gently curved side for concave work.**

HOLD A RIFFLER LIKE A PENCIL. **If you want more control or a heavier cut, press on the end of the head.**

about $25 and is available from Woodcraft (see Sources). Although it's technically a double-cut file (the rows of teeth intersect), each row of teeth is made up of short sections, offset slightly, to minimize clogging.

Rifflers

Rifflers are slender S-shaped tools with rectangular, oval, triangular, and pointed heads. They can be either rasps or files (both are available) and are used primarily for small-scale detail carving. Both ends have teeth, and the most useful offer a coarse end and a fine end on the same tool. Rifflers are usually about 7 in. long and often come in sets of around eight. I use them all the time to remove tool marks and to sharpen carving details.

Using rifflers Rifflers are held in one hand like a pencil. Sometimes the forefinger of the other hand applies light pressure to help control the cutting action.

The heads on rifflers are so small and the teeth so fine that it's almost impossible not to use a short back-and-forth stroke when cutting with them, but you should use the longest stroke you can to take full advantage of the length of the head.

* Please note price estimates are from 1995.

MARIO RODRIGUEZ is a contributing editor to *Fine Woodworking* magazine and the author of *Building Fireplace Mantels* (Taunton Press, 2002).

Sources

Nicholson
A division of
Cooper Tools
P.O. Box 728
Apex, NC 27502
(919) 362-7511

Woodcraft
210 Wood County
Industrial Park
P.O. Box 1686
Parkersburg, WV
26102-1686
(800) 535-4482

Sanding Fids

BY KING HEIPLE

A fid is traditionally a tapered wooden tool that's used by sail makers to stretch holes in canvas or to stretch and size rope grommets. In Italy, furniture makers developed a similarly shaped tool for sanding wood. I saw a picture of a sanding fid a few years ago, and I have since made several versions of this curiously named tool.

Fids turn out to be widely useful in the shop, and making one is a quick and straightforward project, even if you have only very basic wood-turning skills. Fids are particularly useful for sanding carvings, furniture legs, and turnings with varying coves, as well as for fairing one compound cove curve smoothly into another.

As anyone who's used a drum or disc sander knows, supported sandpaper lasts 2 to 10 times longer than handheld sandpaper. Even better, with a fid you can

A FID IS PERFECT FOR SMOOTHING ONE CURVE INTO ANOTHER. The author uses a fid to refine and blend the curved ankle of a curly maple cabriole leg (above). Cementing cork or neoprene on the taper (left) adds pliability and makes it easier to smooth curves.

Making a Fid

You need only basic turning skills to make a sanding fid. The first step is turning the handle. It can be any design that suits you. Once you've turned the handle, work on the tapered portion with a large roughing gouge skewed at 45 degrees. Take a light cut, starting at the tip and gradually backing up (photo 1).

No matter what your desired degree of taper, it's important that it be smooth. Any bump or curve will pre-vent a close fit of the sandpaper, and dips will create unsupported soft spots. As you develop the taper, check the flatness frequently using a straight-edge (photo 2).

It helps to set the lathe's tool rest at the angle you wish to achieve. Then gradually develop your taper parallel to the rest. Take a finishing cut when the taper is essentially complete (photo 3) or finish smoothing with sandpaper.

Turn the corners at the base and tip with a spindle gouge (photo 4), then finish the fid while it's still on the lathe.

The next and last step is to cut the kerf on the bandsaw (photo 5). For safety, grip the handle of the fid with a parallel jaw clamp. Saw as straight as possible up the center of the taper from the tip to the base.

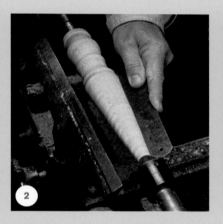

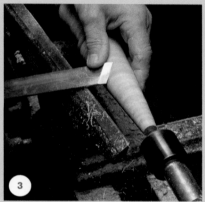

use almost any sandpaper or sanding cloth, without the need for snap locks, hooks and loops, or adhesive backing. And you can change from one grit to another in about 10 seconds.

My fids happen to be cherry, because I like tools to look good and feel nice, but even a construction-grade 2x2 would work fine. The handles can be of any design that meets your fancy, from a straight cylinder to something better than mine. Each of my two longer fids has a 6½-in.-long tapered portion, and my shorter fid has a 3-in.-long tapered portion. The thicker of the long fids tapers from 11/16 in. dia. to 7/16 in. dia.; the thinner one tapers from 11/16 in. dia. to 3/8 in. dia. The short fid is 2¼ in. dia. at its base and tapers ¼ in. over its 3-in. length, about as close to a true cylinder as you can get and still lock on sandpaper tightly.

The degree of taper is not critical, and you may need to turn several variations, but the taper must be uniform—that is to say, flat—or your fid will not hold sandpaper tightly or support it well. Once you have turned the fid on the lathe, go to the bandsaw and cut a kerf exactly down the middle of the fid, from the narrow end of the taper to the handle. Keep the kerf as straight as possible. The kerf may have to be sanded a bit, but slightly rough inner surfaces will help it hold the paper.

A reusable sandpaper pattern is easy to make. Take a piece of paper at least as long as

the taper and wrap it around the fid. Holding the paper snugly, run your thumbnail up the kerf on one side of the taper, and also mark the length of the taper. Unwrap the paper, and you'll have the pattern for your fid, but you must add ⅜ in. to each long side for the fold-in flaps. Now spray the paper pattern with adhesive and mount it on a scrap of plywood or pressboard. Cut this pattern out, sand its edges and label it. Use the pattern to cut a set of sandpaper fid covers in varying grits, and you'll save time in the future. Very lightweight sandpaper (A weight) does not stay on a fid well, but heavier sandpaper and sanding cloth work beautifully.

Lately I've taken to cementing either a ⅛-in. layer of cork or a ⅛-in. neoprene sheet to the taper. Either material adds just enough compliance to the surface to make the sanding of transitions from one curve to another smooth and easy. I suspect there will be those who say, "Just use a dowel or your finger." But I enjoy turning fids. And a fid makes a useful addition to your tool chest and to your vocabulary.

KING HEIPLE is a retired orthopedic surgeon and a lifelong woodworker.

Making Your Own Tools

BY ASA CHRISTIANA

In our travels as *Fine Woodworking* editors, we look over the shoulders of some of the country's best woodworkers. It's one of the reasons why a lot of us took the job. In these working shops, we see which techniques are truly useful and which are a waste of time. The same goes for tools.

Accomplished woodworkers tend to go beyond the tools available in stores and catalogs and simply make or adapt their own. Near almost every benchtop, from Connecticut to Kentucky to California, I find an assortment of shopmade hand tools. Next to gleaming sets of finely manufactured chisels, handplanes, and layout tools, there usually is a small row of makeshift implements, from chisels shaped for a specific task to marking and whittling knives, layout jigs, and other assorted gizmos.

While these handmade tools usually don't represent the height of the toolmaker's art—most would look more at home under a mattress on Riker's Island—their edges are razor sharp and their sometimes crude handles show signs of constant use.

Dovetailing Aids

SHOPMADE DOVETAIL GUIDE. Made of two bits of hardwood, this simple layout guide has given Mark Edmundson years of service.

THIN CHISEL FOR THIN PINS. Edmundson uses this shopmade chisel to clean out the narrow sockets between dovetails.

Sometimes it's simply quicker and easier to find a bit of steel in your shop and create what you need than it is to hunt down the item in a catalog and wait for it to arrive. Certainly it's cheaper. Other times the specialty tool you need simply doesn't exist in today's marketplace.

The ability to imagine and create your own tools when necessary is a matter of confidence and knowing a few metalworking basics. When you learn what you can do with a bench grinder, for instance, new tool ideas will follow.

Finally, we all enjoy creating furniture and other woodwork, and making the tools to do so just takes that sense of creativity and self-reliance one step further.

Edmundson's "Convict Line"

Mark Edmundson, a custom furniture maker in northern Idaho, calls his set of marking knives and specialty chisels his "convict line." Time is money, so the emphasis is on utility over beauty. He made his favorite marking knife from a dull planer blade, first removing the sharp edge with a belt sander, then grinding a sharp bevel on one end and wrapping blue tape around the other end to protect his hand.

Planer and jointer knives make good stock for shopmade tools because they are high-speed steel and don't need to be hardened or tempered after grinding. Just be careful not to overheat them on the grinding wheel. If the steel begins to change color, it's getting too hot. Dunk it often in water, and use a light touch on the wheel.

Edmundson's tool collection also includes two narrow chisels he made from triangular files. He uses the thinnest one to chop out waste in the tight spaces between dovetails. He uses the other, which is narrow rather than thin, when making grooves for stringing. Although the bulk of the narrow grooves are cut using a router with a template-and-bushing setup, the bit leaves round corners. The tiny, narrow chisel quickly squares off these areas.

A custom tool doesn't have to be an edge tool. Edmundson reaches just as often for a simple dovetail guide he made from two scraps of hardwood fit and glued together.

Part Chairmaker, Part Inventor

As woodworkers progress, they gravitate toward favorite designs and techniques. Then, as they repeat tasks again and again, they find points where standard tools fall short. Brian Boggs, a chairmaker in Berea, Ky., has a favorite finishing touch for the pinned mortise-and-tenon joints on the back posts of his chairs. He leaves the pins about ⅛ in. proud and cuts facets into each one, creating a shallow pyramid shape.

Boggs, who works to streamline and perfect every process in his shop, found that

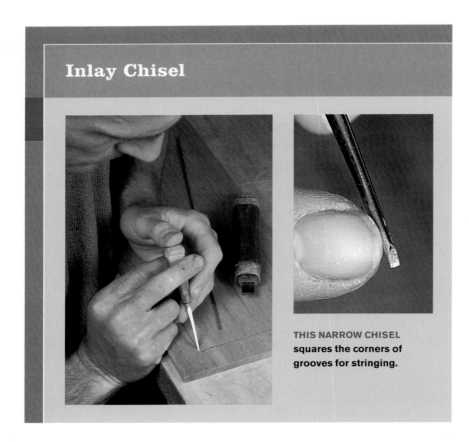

Inlay Chisel

THIS NARROW CHISEL squares the corners of grooves for stringing.

a standard chisel wouldn't do the job properly. He needed a "tight, rotating cut to get into the bottom and up the pyramid" and a "wide bearing surface that wouldn't bruise the wood" as he was levering against it. He ground and polished a round surface onto both sides of a chisel and found he could slice perfect facets every time, from either direction.

Boggs encountered another problem with mortising the thin chair slats into the back posts. He had trouble cleaning out the bottoms of the deep, narrow mortises. He ground a sharp hook onto the bottom of an antique screwdriver, putting the cutting edge at a right angle to the shaft. The finished tool is very similar to the Japanese chisels used to clean out mortises in shoji screens. He didn't need to harden the edge because he uses the tool more like a scoop than a chisel, scraping chips off the bottom and dragging them out of the mortise.

Boggs's ingenuity hasn't stopped at simple hand tools. As he has worked over the years to refine the Appalachian ladder-back form, he has also worked to refine the tools of his trade. His shopmade innovations include a pressurized steam chamber, a curved chairmaker's spokeshave (now available from Lee Valley Tools) and a Rube Goldberg–like machine that takes rough hickory bark in one end and turns out rolls of perfect seat-weaving material on the other, slicing it to uniform width and thickness with a series of oscillating razor blades and jets of lubricating fluid. Boggs designed the machine and then worked with a local machinist to build it. While I may never go this far to refine my craft, examples like Boggs's have inspired me to take greater risks and to venture beyond the tools available in catalogs.

Yankee Ingenuity

Another frequent contributor to the magazine, Philip C. Lowe, who helped develop

A Pair of Chairmaker's Tools

ROUND SIDES FOR FLAT FACETS. By rounding the sides and angling the edge of this chisel, Brian Boggs found he could cut cleaner facets on the ends of his pins. The tool can cut in either direction, pivoting off its round back.

HOOKED CHISEL CLEANS OUT deep, narrow mortises. Boggs made this tool from a screwdriver and uses it to hook and extract chips from the bottom of a mortise (see the top photo on p. 140 for another view of the tool).

the cabinetmaking curriculum at Boston's North Bennet Street School and has hundreds of period reproductions and restorations to his credit, now runs a school of his own in Beverly, Mass. His cabinetmaking students are always curious about the specialty tools Lowe drags out from time to time. Before long they are making their own versions. A favorite is the custom scraper Lowe uses for turning decorative faces on small knobs. Starting with an old file, recent graduate Jason Rivers made a custom tool like this to spruce up one of the required projects, a tool chest. Then, with one plunge cut on the lathe, he cut an

Making a Chisel from a File

J. PETROVICH

A great number of tools can be made by the average woodworker using common materials and equipment. A specialty chisel, for example, can be made using a worn-out file, a bench grinder, and your kitchen oven (think TV's MacGyver).

Files are a good choice for tool stock for three reasons. First of all, they are carbon steel, so they respond to heat treatment, allowing the toolmaker to control the hardness through tempering. Second, files are already fully hardened and require only a moderate heat source (kitchen oven) to make them useful. Third, files come in useful shapes that already suggest their second life: triangular file for a dovetail chisel, heavy wood rasp for a lathe tool, flat file for a custom screwdriver. This reduces grinding time.

Initially, a file is too hard and brittle to make a useful cutting edge. Under any pounding blows the edge would shatter. Tempering the steel trades some of this hardness for toughness. By raising the temperature of the steel to 428°F, the harness is lowered from Rc68 to Rc70 (Rockwell C hardness) to Rc58 to Rc60.

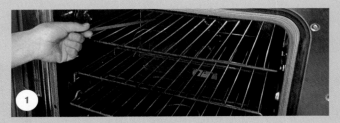

TRADE SOME HARDNESS FOR TOUGHNESS. Placing the file in the oven for one hour at a little over 425°F will temper the steel, making it more suitable for an edge tool.

GRIND AWAY THE FILE TEETH. You can do this freehand, holding the file sideways. Dunk it in water often to keep it from overheating.

Normally a toolmaker would "read" this temperature in the color (a pale straw color, in this case) produced by a heat source on the smooth surface of the steel, but you can control the temperature with the thermostat on the kitchen oven.

Place the file on a rack near the top of the oven. Set tht dial for a little more than 425°F and bake the file for one hour. "Kitchen tempering" complete, the tool blank is ready to grind.

First, grind off the file's teeth and reshape the file slightly. I like to do this grinding without the tool rest, using the bottom side of the wheel. This takes a little practice, but ultimately you will find that you can adjust your body and hands to serve as a very accommodating and accurate jig. Because grinding can produce temperatures high enough to remove the hardness from the

attractive rosette into the face of each knob, each one identical to the rest.

Lowe and his students don't temper the brittle steel of the file after reshaping it on the grinding wheel because it doesn't take as much shock and stress as a chisel does.

Only ½ in. of the tool should hang over the lathe's tool rest—not enough to snap it off.

Some of the most helpful tools in Lowe's shopmade collection are the simplest. His drawerful of sanding dowels is an example. He uses them to sand cove moldings and cuts off one end of each dowel at a edge, I do not wear gloves. Bare hands are very sensitive to temperatures above 100°F and tell me when the temperature is too high. Keep a cup of water handy for cooling the tool (and your fingers), and use it often.

When the grinding is done, you can flatten the surface further with a file. A smoother surface still can be made with progressive grades of wet-or-dry sandpaper using a light oil or thinner for lubricant.

Remount the grinder's tool rest and establish a cutting edge as you normally would. Handles for these tools can be made from almost any scrap of hardwood. Shape it to taste and comfort. Because the file already has a tang for mount-

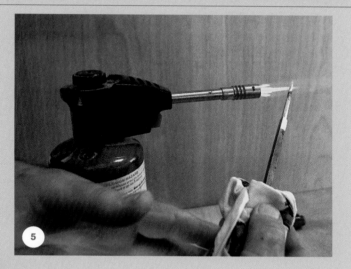

ATTACH A HANDLE. Drill a stepped hole in the handle and heat the tang. The hot metal will burn its way into the hole for a tight fit.

ing, little more is required than drilling the handle to accommodate the tang. The hole should be stepped smaller at the bottom. Open up the hole until you can insert half to two-thirds of the tang into the hole. Then wrap the blade portion of the tool in a wet washcloth and heat the bottom quarter of the tang using a propane torch or a gas flame on the kitchen stove until it glows very slightly. Next, insert the tang into the handle as far as you can, then tap the end of the handle with a small hammer. Should this fail, let everything cool and drill the hole larger. Should you go too large, set the tang with epoxy.

J. Petrovich is a furniture maker in Slinas, California.

SMOOTH THE SURFACES WITH A FILE. A normal file will cut your tool blank, which has been softened slightly.

GRIND THE CHISEL TIP. A tool rest helps at this point to establish an even bevel. Use a light touch when grinding, and cool the tool down.

45 degree angle so that he can reach into inside corners.

Usually, the time it takes to make a custom tool is negligible compared to the time and effort it will save you. All it takes is the confidence to try. Once you've solved a problem with a shopmade tool, other tools and gizmos will follow. And because you made them, they'll look as attractive hanging on your wall as your set of $200 chisels.

ASA CHRISTIANA is the managing editor of *Fine Woodworking* magazine.

Get a Grip on Your Tools

BY
CHRISTIAN H.
BECKSVOORT

I had my dovetail saw for some time before I gave it its first real workout. I was making a large case piece with almost 400 hand-cut dovetails. Halfway through the first day of sawing, I began to notice blisters forming. I realized my high-priced, brass-backed, British dovetail saw needed some serious customizing if I was ever to finish the piece. Out came the knife, rasp, file, sandpaper, and gouge. I then chopped and carved the handle until it fit my hand. A little more scraping and sanding followed by a coat of oil completed the project.

In about an hour, I had converted the stock saw handle from a painful tool into one that I look forward to using because it fits like a glove. But if your stock handle is beyond hope or just plain ugly, another option is to start from scratch and create a unique custom handle for your saw, as discussed in the sidebar on pp. 144–145.

A tool handle is the link between you and the tool. This is where control takes place. If the hand is not perfectly comfortable and at ease, then you lose some of that control. Consequently, a well-fitted handle can make you a better woodworker.

That saw was my first venture into customizing handles, which has since spread throughout my toolbox (see the bottom

photo on the facing page). Since that time I have modified or replaced handles on tools such as chisels, planes, drills and braces, clamps, and screwdrivers.

The decision of whether to modify or replace is an individual one. I have an aversion to plastic handles. They get replaced immediately. I also dislike garish bright paint and tinted lacquer. For instance, I scraped and sanded off the finish on my wood-handled screwdrivers, and in the process I also filed and sanded their rough ends. Carving tools received the same treatment. Anyone who has ever held a gouge for more than 10 minutes can appreciate the comfort of a smooth, rounded handle end against the palm.

I couldn't find a wood-handled, square-drive screwdriver, so I salvaged the wooden handle from a worn-out Phillips-head

MAKING A NEW TOOL HANDLE doesn't take a lot of time, and the benefits are well worth it. A new handle will make the tool more comfortable and easier to control, contributing to better woodworking.

screwdriver. The wooden handle pulled off the shaft relatively easily, but I had to cut the plastic handle off the square-drive screwdriver using a worn-out blade on the bandsaw. I then drove the square-drive's shaft into the salvaged wooden handle.

Rehandling Planes

Years ago, planes had rosewood handles and knobs, then walnut, then stained beech or birch, and now many handles are plastic. The rosewood handles I leave alone, and I usually don't change walnut handles unless they're damaged. But I do replace the others. I usually turn a new front knob first. The existing knob is a rough guide, but now's the time to adapt it to your grip. The only fixed diameter is where the knob mates to the plane body.

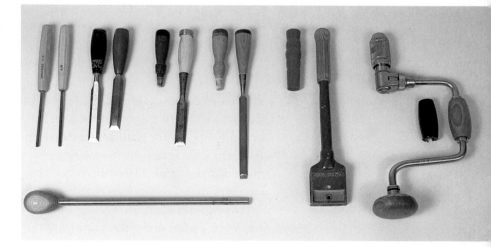

REHANDLING A SHOPFUL OF TOOLS. Shown here are before (on the left) and after examples of tools that have modified or new handles. From the left, Pfeil™ carving gouges (edges eased and sanded), Stanley No. 40 chisels (handle replaced, new steel cap), Stanley No. 750 socket chisels (handle replaced, stainless steel hoop), Greenlee chisel (handle reshaped), Allway® Tools scraper (handle replaced), Stanley No. 923 brace (handles replaced), shopmade lathe knock-out bar with black locust knob.

Regrip Your Saws

MARIO RODRIGUEZ

We've all admired the beautiful handles on antique woodworking saws. Their flourishes, rooster tails, and swirling cusps suggest movement and speed. Usually made of beech, apple, or pear, these handles are minor works of art. Today, most saws are fitted with blister-raising slabs of wood that cramp the hand and fatigue the arm.

A custom handle will improve the performance as well as the look of your saw. A comfortable and properly shaped grip makes it easier to guide the saw for more accurate cuts and excellent results.

Choosing your material: Handle making requires only a small piece of wood, so you might as well use some wildly spectacular stock. I've salvaged most of my handle stock from the scrap bin or firewood pile. Start with a piece of ⅞-in.-thick unusual or figured wood that's about 6 in. by 7 in., orienting the grain lengthwise.

Choosing a handle pattern: Small backsaws have pistol-grip handles. Large backsaws and full-length handsaws usually have closed or hollow handles. I have six handle patterns I use, and I'm always looking for new ones. I frequently make tracings of interesting designs. Sometimes I copy a design from an old tool catalog and have it enlarged. Experiment and anticipate changing the handle more than once until you find a grip that works for you. A good design evolves after some use and time for evaluation.

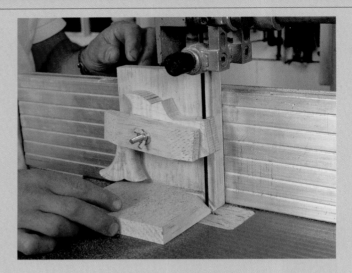

A SPECIAL JIG HOLDS THE HANDLE BLANK when bandsawing the sawblade kerf. Although a bandsaw kerf is slightly oversized, it doesn't affect the final fit of blade to handle.

A pistol-grip pattern is easy to make and will work for most small backsaws measuring 8 in. to 12 in. long. The shape is easy to cut out. There are no interior cuts, and it can be done on the bandsaw.

A closed or hollow handle requires an interior cutout. First drill pilot holes and then complete the cut on a scroll- or jigsaw. Or you can cut the blank into two pieces, make your interior cutout, and reglue and complete your exterior silhouette.

To drill the centered, counterbored hole into the top of the round knob, I first clamp a piece of scrapwood to the drill-press table. Then I drill a flat-bottomed hole, the same diameter as the knob base, about ¼ in. deep into the scrapwood. I change bits to fit the bolt head, place the knob in the hole, and drill the countersink for the bolt head. The depth is critical to get the bolt perfectly flush with the sur-

rounding knob. Finally, I change bits again and drill for the bolt shaft. Then all the knob needs is a little oil and it's ready to screw onto the plane.

The back handle or tote is just as easy. I bandsaw the rough shape, drill the counter-sunk hole for the long bolt, and then shape the handle to suit with a rasp, file, and sandpaper. I carved the last handle I made, as shown in the top photo on p. 143 and left the

Shaping the handle: You can quickly round corners using a table-mounted router with a ball bearing–guided bit. Taking several shallow cuts, round the interior cutout and the back of the grip. Don't eliminate the flat surfaces. A handle that is too round tends to be slippery. For the rooster tail, I prefer a thumbnail profile cut by hand with chisels and files. Try for crisp, sharp edges.

Plotting the cut for the sawblade: Lay the sawblade onto your handle. Mark the top and bottom corners of the sawblade onto the handle and draw a line connecting the two. This should be the baseline of the cut into the handle for the blade.

I usually pitch the handle forward at 50 degrees to 60 degrees in relation to the cutting edge, as opposed to the stock angle of about 70 degrees. This helps me to direct the force of my stroke directly behind the blade for easier, more controlled cutting.

Cutting the blade slot: For speed and accuracy, I usually cut the slot on a bandsaw fitted with a ¼-in.-wide, 6-teeth-per-inch blade. Although a bandsaw leaves a kerf wider than the thickness of the handsaw blade, the difference is negligible and ultimately will not affect the fit of the blade. For safety, I use a jig (see the photo on the facing page) to securely hold the handle with the blade slot baseline parallel to the bandsaw blade.

I sometimes cut the slot by hand for a tighter fit. I use the saw to be rehandled with the old handle reattached temporarily. However, this method requires extreme care, because if your cut is off line it will force a kink into your blade when you fit it to the handle.

Spine mortise: If you're working with a backsaw, you'll have to cut a narrow open-ended mortise into the top of your handle to accommodate the spine. Mark on each side of the blade slot for the width of the spine, and carry the mark down the front of the handle. Cut the sides of the mortise with a small dovetail saw, and then carefully pare out the waste with a ¼-in. chisel. Periodically set the blade into the handle to check for fit. Cut this mortise on the small side and enlarge as necessary to avoid any gaps in the finished job.

Drilling the holes: Make a cardboard template of the heel end of the blade, including the blade holes. Line up the template to the blade baseline drawn on the handle. Drill the screw and nut holes slightly oversized for an easy fit. For a cleaner look, you should countersink the saw nuts almost flush with the handle.

Finishing the handle: After sanding with 320-grit paper, I spray a light coat of lacquer sander/sealer, followed by a coat of gloss lacquer. Sometimes I brush on two coats of shellac instead. When dry, rub the finish with 0000 steel wool, then wax.

facets (see the photo on p. 142). I liked the look of the carved handle, and I thought the hewn texture would improve the grip. Finally, I drill the hole for the short, front-mounting bolt. After a coat of oil, I attach the handle to the plane. As with other handles, I add a few more coats of oil over the next few days.

Turning Chisel Handles

My first effort involved a set of Greenlee socket chisels, which I reshaped by chucking the tapered end of the handle into a three-jaw chuck on my lathe. I turned the handles into smooth cones with a gentle curve and sanded and finished them in a few minutes.

New socket handles are almost as easy to make. I cut my rough stock to 1½-in.-sq.

blanks, 6 in. long, and place it into my toaster oven (set to 200°F) for one or two days. This dries the wood to 0 percent moisture content. Then I turn the blank to shape and cut a taper on one end to fit the chisel's socket. I turn the other end for a stainless-steel hoop to prevent the handle from splitting when hit with a mallet. I prefer stainless steel to brass or copper for hoops because it doesn't tarnish, and the silver color goes well with any wood. I buy ¾-in.-ID stainless pipe at a local machine shop, have them cut it to ⅜-in. lengths, and radius the edges of the resulting hoops. I then polish the hoops before fitting them to the handle.

It's important to turn the handle to fit the hoop immediately after drying and to have the hoops on hand to test the fit. If you get a good, snug fit at this stage, when the wood returns to equilibrium moisture content it will swell and securely anchor the hoop.

Tang chisels are even easier. I select the stock and drill the hole for the tang. The hole should be undersized to get a good fit. The only critical dimension on the turning is at the bottom to accommodate the ferrule, either salvaged or new, that keeps the handle from splitting when the tang is forced into the handle.

Split-Handle Installations

My most challenging handle replacement was for a set of Stanley No. 40 chisels. The handles on these chisels consist of a metal strike cap on top of a 1-in.-dia. metal shaft that was forced into the top of a hollow polycarbonate handle. The chisel shaft was forced into the other end of the handle until it met the strike-cap shaft. It does not require an advanced degree in metallurgy to figure out that two pieces of steel shaft forced against each other by constant pounding will eventually mushroom. Indeed, one handle in my set would split

every three to six months. I would send the chisel back to Stanley and they would dutifully send me a new one.

They stopped making the No. 40s in the late 1970s. At that point, I bandsawed the plastic handles off and pondered a solution. I had a machinist friend and neighbor turn new strike caps with long, oversized shafts, which he drilled out to accept the chisel shafts. I took a wooden blank, cut straight at both ends to the correct length. Then I drilled it from the top to accept the strike cap sleeve and from the bottom to accept the remaining chisel shaft. Next I turned the handle to approximate the old plastic handle. After oiling the hollow handle, I took a wide chisel and split it lengthwise. Finally, I epoxied and clamped the two halves around the shafts of the chisel and strike cap. With a little more sanding and oiling, the split line is virtually invisible. I used the same split handle technique to replace the plastic handle on the swing arm of a brace after bandsawing off the old handle.

Rehandling Machines

Wooden handles on stationary power tools are a pleasure to use. For odd-size bars or control levers, I usually drill the mounting hole into my wooden handle blank the next larger size, turn the knob, and epoxy it into place. For screw-on knobs, I use threaded brass inserts of the correct size, fitted into the knob.

CHRISTIAN H. BECKSVOORT builds custom furniture in New Gloucester, Maine, and is a contributing editor to *Fine Woodworking* magazine.

Chisel Handles
to Order

W oodworkers who visit my shop always ask how I have managed to find such a large variety of chisels with matching handles. And they always want to know what kind of wood the handles are made of. The answer is I make my own handles, and I mainly use wood from cutoffs pulled out of my scrap

BY MARIO RODRIGUEZ

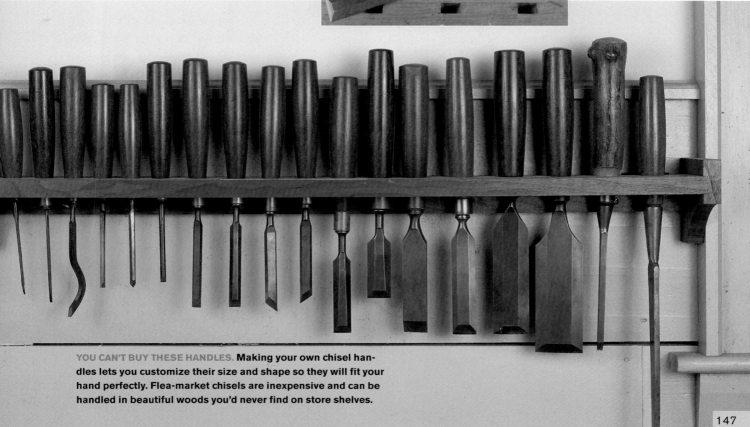

YOU CAN'T BUY THESE HANDLES. Making your own chisel handles lets you customize their size and shape so they will fit your hand perfectly. Flea-market chisels are inexpensive and can be handled in beautiful woods you'd never find on store shelves.

bin. I've pulled some really spectacular pieces of wood from my firewood pile.

Making my own chisel handles lets me customize their size and shape. The result is a tool that looks and works better. Making my own handles also lets me have my pick of all those unhandled antique chisels and gouges that everyone else passes up at flea markets and yard sales (see the photos on p. 147).

Rehandling a chisel is much less of a project than most woodworkers realize. It doesn't take a machinist's precision to make a handle that stays on. A few rough measurements, a good eye, and a test-fit or two will get you there. And it only takes a half-hour or less to make, finish, and attach a handle.

Chisels Have Sockets or Tangs

Although there's a chisel for every imaginable woodworking task, all chisels have either a socket or a tang. You'll find more socket than tang chisels at flea markets and used-tool sales. Socket chisels used to be the standard, but they're not made much now.

A socket is simply a conical recess in the steel. One end of the handle is tapered to a cone that mates with the socket. A friction fit holds the chisel and handle together. Pounding on the back end of the chisel seats the handle more tightly, so socket chisels are well-suited for chopping as well as paring.

Most modern bench chisels and gouges are made with a tang. This is a tapered projection, usually about 1¼ in. long, that mates with a centered hole in the handle. These chisels are great for paring, but they should not be used for any heavy chopping because the tang can split the handle.

Making the Handles

Initially, making a handle for both socket and tang chisels is the same. Determine a

length and a diameter for the handle and prepare a blank to those dimensions. Adding a few extra inches to the blank will make turning easier. If you're turning a handle for a socket chisel, don't forget to include the part that fits inside the socket.

Think about the size of the blade and how that will affect the balance of the chisel. Consider the chisel's intended use. I make a short, thin handle for a chisel that has a narrow blade because this chisel does more delicate work. On my firmer chisel, which I use for chopping, I made a long, beefy handle. It will stand up to more abuse and will help counterbalance the weight of the blade.

Start by marking the center of the blank at both ends; diagonals from corner to corner will cross at the center. Remove the drive center from the headstock of your lathe and center its point on the center of the blank. Tap the blank a few times with a hammer, just enough so the spurs bite well but not enough to split the blank. Now chuck the blank in your lathe and position the tailstock.

Using a roughing gouge and then a shallower gouge will take the blank to the approximate shape you want (see photo 1 on the facing page). Use a pencil line to mark all transitional locations and come back with a parting tool. You'll want to mark the point where either the socket or ferrule starts, as well as the actual tail end of the chisel (see photo 2 on on the facing page). On more complicated chisel patterns, mark the locations of beads, coves, and other details.

Socket chisels If you're rehandling a socket chisel, turn the cone to rough dimension now. I use a carpenter's rule held above the spinning blank to estimate diameter. You might prefer calipers. Keep the cone about ⅛ in. shorter than the socket depth, so it won't bottom out. Clear away some space on the waste side of the tail end

Grip and Stance

1. USE A ROUGHING GOUGE TO TURN THE BLANK TO APPROXIMATE SHAPE. Then take a shallower gouge to smooth the blank. Position the tool rest as close to the blank as you can; move it in as you remove material.

2. MARK TRANSITIONS WITH A PENCIL AND THEN A PARTING TOOL. The pencil mark on the right is where the cone will start. The part on the left defines the tail end of the chisel.

3. ROUND OVER THE TAIL END OF THE CHISEL. Clear some space on the waste side of the part first, though, so your gouge won't catch. Turn the cone to rough dimension.

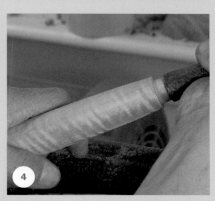

4. TEST-FIT CONE TO SOCKET. A snug fit with about ⅛-in. space between the shoulder and the end of the socket is what you're after. This one is still a little too tight.

5. DIRT AND BURNISHED AREAS MARK HIGH SPOTS. Rechuck the handle, remove more material, and check the fit again. Repeat until the fit is right.

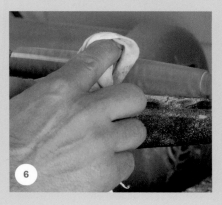

6. PUT ON A COAT OF FINISH. Padding lac- quer, which is the author's choice, goes on quickly and dries almost immediately.

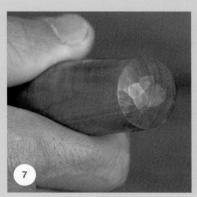

7. A FACETED END can be a nice custom touch.

Tang Handle

1. SNEAK UP ON A PERFECT FIT. Make the section for the ferrule twice as long as it needs to be, turn the end smaller than the inside diameter of the ferrule, and keep parting away the section near the shoulder until the ferrule fits.

2. DRILL A HOLE FOR THE TANG. Replace the center in your tailstock with a chuck. Use a brad-point bit about the size of the tang or a little smaller. Center the point of the bit and advance the tailstock slowly as the lathe runs.

3. PARE OR FILE THE HOLE IN THE END OF THE HANDLE until the tang fits. Or you can use a drill with a bit in it as a power rasp. Don't remove too much material, or the handle will split.

of the chisel, and then round over the tail end with a small gouge (see photo 3 on p. 149).

Remove the chisel handle from the lathe and check the fit of the cone in the socket (see photo 4 on p. 149). You're looking for a snug fit that takes a fair amount of effort to seat. You won't get this fit right away, but you'll know what to remove by looking for shiny or dirty spots on the cone when you remove the socket (see photo 5 on p. 149). When test-fitting the handle to the blade, look for about ³⁄₁₆ in. to ¼ in. between the socket and the shoulder of the handle (when the handle is finished and you've driven it home onto the blade, there should be a gap of about ⅛ in.). Rechuck the blank, use a gouge or parting tool to remove a little material from the cone, and test the fit again. Repeat until the fit is right.

Sand to 320-grit and then burnish with some of the chips and shavings you've just removed. This will start to bring up a shine. For a finish, I use Qualasole, a padding lacquer made by Behlen (sold through Garrett Wade and Woodworker's supply). I just pour a little on a T-shirt scrap, apply it while the lathe is spinning and I'm done (see photo 6 on p. 149). The finish dries in a minute or two.

Remove the handle from the lathe, clamp the chisel blade firmly into a vise, and hammer the handle home. A little duct tape around the blade will help prevent it from slipping or being damaged if you're clamping it in a metalworking vise. Saw off the excess blank and pare, file, or sand the end until you're happy with it. The end of the handle can be made perfectly smooth like the rest of the handle or faceted so there's some texture (see photo 7 on p. 149).

Tang chisels The major difference between rehandling socket and tang chisels is that a tang chisel requires a ferrule. The ferrule, simply a metal ring around the handle where the tang enters it, helps prevent the chisel handle from splitting. I make ferrules from brass, or more commonly, copper plumbing pipe. Don't use a hacksaw to cut the pipe or you'll distort the ferrule. Use a pipe cutter instead and you'll have a ferrule that will go on easily.

I make the end of the chisel where the ferrule sits twice as long as it will be on the finished chisel. This extra length gives me a place to hold the ferrule as I turn the spot where the ferrule will sit to the proper diameter. This allows me to sneak up on a perfect fit (see photo 1 on the facing page).

After getting the ferrule snugly onto the end of the handle, finish turning the blank to shape and sand, burnish, and finish it just like the socket chisel. I file the end of the ferrule to remove any burrs and to give the end a nicely beveled appearance.

Remove the lathe's tail center and replace it with a tailstock chuck and a bit that's about the same diameter as the tang. I use a brad-point bit because I can center the point on the depression left by the tail center. Advance the tailstock slowly into the end of the handle while supporting the handle with your other hand (see photo 2 on the facing page). If I can't advance the tailstock far enough, I'll cut off some of the excess where I held the ferrule. Then I'll repeat the drilling process after moving the tailstock closer.

After drilling the hole just a little deeper than the tang is long (so it doesn't bottom out and split the handle), remove the handle from the lathe, saw off the excess at the blade end, and square up and expand the hole until the tang fits snugly (see photo 3 on the facing page). If the tang is too loose, use shims to tighten it. When you have the fit you want, clean up the end and you're done.

MARIO RODRIGUEZ is a contributing editor to *Fine Woodworking* magazine and the author of *Building Fireplace Mantels* (Taunton Press, 2002).

Credits

The articles in this book appeared in the following issues of *Fine Woodworking*:

p. 4: Four Tools You Shouldn't Overlook by Mike Dunbar, issue 150. Photos on p. 4 by Erika Marks, courtesy *Fine Woodworking*, © The Taunton Press, Inc.,except photos on pp. 5-7 by Asa Christiana, courtesy *Fine Woodworking*, © The Taunton Press, Inc.

p. 8: Shop on the Go by Mario Rodriguez, issue 153. Photos by Michael Pekovich, courtesy *Fine Woodworking*, © The Taunton Press, Inc.

p. 15: How to Buy Used Hand Tools by Robert Hubert Jr., issue 98. Photos by Alec Waters, courtesy *Fine Woodworking*, © The Taunton Press, Inc., except photo on p. 19 by Beryl Goldberg, courtesy *Fine Woodworking*, © The Taunton Press, Inc. and photo on p. 20 by Susan Kahn, courtesy *Fine Woodworking*, © The Taunton Press, Inc.

p. 22: Buying the Best by Scott Gibson, issue 113. Photos by Boyd Hagen, courtesy *Fine Woodworking*, © The Taunton Press, Inc., except photo on p. 24 by Scott Gibson, courtesy *Fine Woodworking*, © The Taunton Press, Inc.

p. 30: Four-Squaring with Hand Tools by Anthony Guidice, issue 142. Photos by Vicki Guidice, courtesy *Fine Woodworking*, © The Taunton Press, Inc.

p. 34: Bench-Chisel Techniques by Garrett Hack, issue 150. Photos by Michael Pekovich, courtesy *Fine Woodworking*, © The Taunton Press, Inc., except photos on p. 36 (top left and right), p. 37, and p. 39. by Mark Schofield, courtesy *Fine Woodworking*, © The Taunton Press, Inc.

p. 40: Backsaw Workshop by Philip C. Lowe, issuee156. Photos by Timothy Sans. Drawings by Bob La Pointe, courtesy *Fine Woodworking*, © The Taunton Press, Inc.

p. 46: Accurate Joinery Starts with a Marking Knife by Mario Rodriguez, issue 155. Photos by Asa Christiana, courtesy *Fine Woodworking*, © The Taunton Press, Inc. Drawings by Michael Pekovich, courtesy *Fine Woodworking*, © The Taunton Press, Inc.

p. 50: Hammers and Mallets by Mario Rodriguez, issue 160. Photos by Kathleen Williams, courtesy *Fine Woodworking*, © The Taunton Press, Inc.

p. 53: A Basic Layout Kit by Horst J. Meister, issue 121. Photos by Strother Purdy, courtesy *Fine Woodworking*, © The Taunton Press, Inc.

p. 60: The Combination Square: A Perfect Name for a Near Perfect Tool by Anthony Guidice, issue 135. Photos by Jefferson Kolle, courtesy *Fine Woodworking*, © The Taunton Press, Inc., except photo on p. 60 by Michael Pekovich, courtesy *Fine Woodworking*, © The Taunton Press, Inc.

p. 64: Shopmade Squares by Gary Williams, issue 149. Photos by Tom Begnal, courtesy *Fine Woodworking*, © The Taunton Press, Inc. Drawings by Vince Babak, courtesy *Fine Woodworking*, © The Taunton Press, Inc.

p. 72: Shopmade Marging Gauge by John Nesset, issue 150. Photos by Asa Christiana, courtesy *Fine Woodworking*, © The Taunton Press, Inc.

p. 78: Scratch Awl from Scrap by Tom Herold, issue 100. Photo by Susan Kahn, courtesy *Fine Woodworking*, © The Taunton Press, Inc.

p. 82: Story Sticks Leave Little Room for Error by Mario Rodriguez, issue 152. Photo by Kelly J. Dunton, courtesy *Fine Woodworking*, © The Taunton Press, Inc. Drawings by Vince Babak, courtesy *Fine Woodworking*, © The Taunton Press, Inc.

p. 85: Three Everyday Chisels by Sven Hanson, issue 124. Photos by Anatole Burkin, courtesy *Fine Woodworking*, © The Taunton Press, Inc., except photos on pp. 87 and 88 by Alec Waters, courtesy *Fine Woodworking*, © The Taunton Press, Inc. Drawings by Jim Richey, courtesy *Fine Woodworking*, © The Taunton Press, Inc

p. 91: Japanese Chisels by William Tandy Young, issue 115. Photos by Alec Waters, courtesy *Fine Woodworking*, © The Taunton Press, Inc. Drawings by Michael Gellatly, courtesy *Fine Woodworking*, © The Taunton Press, Inc

p.96: Choosing and Using Japanese Handsaws by Toshio Odate, issue 101. Photos by Sandor Nagyszalanczy, courtesy *Fine Woodworking*, © The Taunton Press, Inc. Drawing by Kathleen Rushton, courtesy *Fine Woodworking*, © The Taunton Press, Inc.

p. 102: Soup Up a Dovetail Saw by Mario Rodriguez, issue 121. Photos by Vincent Laurence, courtesy *Fine Woodworking*, © The Taunton Press, Inc.

p. 107: Sharpening Handsaws by Fred Wilder, issue 125. Photos by Strother Purdy, courtesy *Fine Woodworking*, © The Taunton Press, Inc. Drawings by Vince Babak, courtesy *Fine Woodworking*, © The Taunton Press, Inc.

p. 113: The Backsaw Makes a Comeback by Zachary Gaulkin, issue 129. Photos by Scott Phillips, courtesy *Fine Woodworking*, © The Taunton Press, Inc., except photos on p. 113 and 117 by Zachary Gaulkin, courtesy *Fine Woodworking*, © The Taunton Press, Inc.

p. 120: Build a Bowsaw by J. Crate Larkin, issue 151. Photos by Tom Begnal, courtesy *Fine Woodworking*, © The Taunton Press, Inc. Drawings by Bob LaPointe, courtesy *Fine Woodworking*, © The Taunton Press, Inc.

p. 126: Simple Tools Can Reproduce Most Mouldings by Robert S. Judd, issue 109. Photos by Charley Robinson, courtesy *Fine Woodworking*, © The Taunton Press, Inc.

p. 129: Files, Rasps, and Rifflers by Mario Rodriguez, issue 113. Photos by Vincent Laurence, courtesy *Fine Woodworking*, © The Taunton Press, Inc.

p. 134: Sanding Fids by King Heiple, issue 136. Photos by Ernie Conover.

p. 137: Make Your Own Tols by Asa Christiana, issue 153. Photos by Asa Christiana, courtesy *Fine Woodworking*, © The Taunton Press, Inc. except left photo on p. 139 by Kelly J. Dunton, courtesy *Fine Woodworking*, © The Taunton Press, Inc.

p. 142: Get a Grip on Your Tools by Christian H. Becksvoort, issue 105. Photos by Charley Robinson, courtesy *Fine Woodworking*, © The Taunton Press, Inc.

p. 147: Chisel Handles to Order by Mario Rodriguez, issue 120. Photos by Vincent Laurence, courtesy *Fine Woodworking*, © The Taunton Press, Inc.

The New Best of Fine Woodworking series

A collection of the best articles from the last ten years of Fine Woodworking.

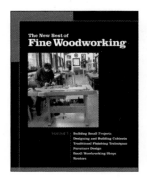

BOBO'S MAGIC WISHES

A STORY FROM PUERTO RICO

Retold by Janet Palazzo-Craig   Illustrated by Charles Reasoner

THIS BOOK IS THE PROPERTY OF:

STATE	Book No.
PROVINCE	Enter information
COUNTY	in spaces
PARISH	to the left as
SCHOOL DISTRICT	instructed.
OTHER	

ISSUED TO	Year Used	CONDITION	
		ISSUED	RETURNED

PUPILS to whom this textbook is issued must not write on any page or mark any part of it in any way, consumable textbooks excepted.

1. Teachers should see that the pupil's name is clearly written in ink in the spaces above in every book issued.
2. The following terms should be used in recording the condition of the book: New; Good; Fair; Poor; Bad.